ANTWERP, A METROPOLIS

This publication appears as part
of ANTWERP 93 Cultural Capital of Europe,
as a result of the exhibition
'Antwerp, Story of a Metropolis
(16th-17th Centuries)'
Hessenhuis, June 25-October 10, 1993

*Cover:*
A. Mor van Dashorst,
Portrait of Sir Thomas Gresham,
(1519-1579), Amsterdam, Rijksmuseum.

# Antwerp, a Metropolis in Comparative Perspective

by PETER BURKE

*Cultural capital of Europe*

# Introduction

In his well-known history of material culture and the rise of commercial capitalism, the great French historian Fernand Braudel distinguished a series of what he called "world economies" in early modern Europe, each dominated by a city: Venice, Antwerp, Genoa, Amsterdam, London.[1] He was concerned with a new form of what the humanists called the *Translatio imperii* (the transfer of power from Persia to Greece, Rome and Germany), in other words with the shift in economic hegemony from one European city to another, especially during the rise of the capitalist "world economy" in the course of the sixteenth century.

This world economy, in which the trading connexions between different parts of the globe became closer than ever before, was based on the division of labour between an economic centre, or "core", and a periphery. The periphery, located in Eastern Europe and the New World, produced raw materials at a low price thanks to the labour of underpaid or unpaid serfs and slaves. The centre, located in Western Europe, imported raw materials and exported manufactured goods, notably textiles. The centre of that centre was always a trading city.[2]

The first world economy in Europe, according to Braudel, was Venice in the age of the Renaissance, a time when the city was closely linked to other leading commercial centres such as Bruges, London, Lisbon, Fez, Damascus and Azov. Venice owed this central position to its favourable location and also to the policies of its government, an oligarchy of merchant-nobles or noble merchants. Bruges, by contrast, was what Braudel calls a "world market", a locale for international trade but not a "sun" at the centre of an economic universe.[3] The position of Venice was gradually undermined by the expansion of the Ottoman Empire in the east, which made trade more difficult, and in the west the rise of a Portuguese seaborne empire which competed with Venice for international trade (most obviously in spices).[4]

However, the city which benefited most from Portuguese expansion was not Lisbon (although it did indeed grow in this period). Instead it was Antwerp, which prospered in the early sixteenth century on the profits of the spice trade (of which it was given the monopoly by the Portuguese Crown in 1503), followed by the trade in the silver which the Spaniards were in the process of extracting from the mines of Mexico and Peru. Antwerp's dominance was short-lived, however. The city was already eclipsed by Genoa in the 1550s (according to Braudel), in other words before the revolt of the Netherlands, let alone the blockade of the river Scheldt by Holland and Zeeland.

One might have expected the role of Antwerp to be taken over by Seville, the growing port through which the silver minted in the New World, from Zacatecas to Potosí, was channelled into Europe via the *Casa de Contratación* or "House of Trade", founded in 1503. Between 1503 and 1660 about 16,000,000 kilograms of silver arrived in Seville, while the city grew from about 60,000 people in 1500 to about 150,000 by 1588. However, it was the Genoese who managed to control that silver, thanks to the services which the city's bankers provided for successive kings of Spain, and the commercial privileges which they exacted in return.[5] As the seventeenth-century Spanish poet Francisco Quevedo put it, in his usual sardonic manner, "Mr Money is a powerful gentleman" [*Poderoso caballero es Don Dinero*]. Born in the Indies, he dies in Spain, but it is in Genoa, according to Quevedo, that Don Dinero is buried.

Like the dominance of Antwerp, the so-called "Age of the Genoese" was relatively brief (from the 1550s to the 1620s, when the city's elite ceased lending money to the king of Spain), and it was followed in turn by the well-known economic hegemony of seventeenth-century Amsterdam. The dominant position of Amsterdam was originally based on the Baltic trade, the "mother trade" as the Dutch used to call it. However, the commercial hinterland or empire of Amsterdam expanded rapidly from the late sixteenth century onwards (partly at the expense of Antwerp), to include the Mediterranean, the East Indies and even the Americas, from Recife in the north-east of Brazil to what is now New York, but was originally known as New Amsterdam.[6] Amsterdam is the last example in Braudel's sequence because its successors, like Britain in the age of the Industrial revolution, were not cities but national economies.

Like Braudel's study, this essay is concerned with a sequence of major cities and their influence in Europe and beyond in the sixteenth, seventeenth and eighteenth centuries. The point of view from which it is written, on the other hand, is somewhat different. It is that of a cultural rather than an economic historian. In other words, the essay deals with a new form of what the humanists called the *Translatio Studii,* the transfer of learning from Athens to Rome, Paris and so on.

In this essay, however, "culture" will not be defined in terms of learning alone. The term will be employed in these pages to refer not only to works of so-called "high" or "elite" culture in literature, music and the visual arts, but to a much wider range of artifacts and performances. Both learned and popular culture will be discussed here, the high and the low, the communication of information by word of mouth (sung as well as spoken), by means of images, and via rituals and other performances, as well as in writing and in print.

The term "city" may also be in need of some preliminary clarification. By the standards of the sixteenth and seventeenth centuries, a major urban centre was one with a population of around 100,000 people. In 1500 there were probably only four cities of this size in Europe: Paris, Venice, Naples and Istanbul. Antwerp reached this figure briefly in the middle of the sixteenth century. By 1600 there were twelve European cities of 100,000 or more, adding to the previous four London, Lisbon, Seville, Milan, Rome, Palermo, Messina, and Moscow, a number which remained more or less constant throughout the seventeenth century (though Amsterdam joined the group), but rose to more than twenty by the end of the eighteenth century. However, as this brief survey will attempt to show, at this time a city with no more than 50,000 or 60,000 inhabitants (sixteenth-century Florence, Rome or Lyons, for example), might still play a major cultural role in Europe.[7]

The term "metropolis" was occasionally applied to some of these cities in the early modern period itself. The word was sometimes used in an ecclesiastical sense, to refer to the seat of the most important bishopric in a particular region; sometimes, following the classical tradition, to describe the mother city of a colony; but also to mean a central point. Thus Venice was described by a foreign visitor in 1567 as the "metropolis of news", while Antwerp was described in

1549, again by a foreigner, as "the metropolis of the world."[8]

The traditional description of Rome as *caput mundi* had a similar meaning, and a number of early modern cities claimed to be a "New Rome", – fifteenth-century Venice, for instance, sixteenth-century Seville, and seventeenth-century Paris.[9] Today, geographers tend to use the term "metropolis" not only to refer to a large city, but – moving from quantity to quality – to describe a major city which embodies what is most distinctive in the culture of its region.[10]

In this comparative essay I should like to use the phrase "cultural metropolis" somewhat more precisely than early modern travellers – and even contemporary geographers – to refer to any city which functioned as the central place of a large region (Western Europe, if not Europe as a whole), and performed this function – if not for the whole range of culture – at least for some major cultural activities.

For example, certain university cities – Bologna, Padua, Paris, Oxford, Leiden – fit this definition, since they attracted students from a large area; Englishmen studied in Padua, Hungarians in Oxford, Poles in Leiden, and so on. Students from the periphery of Europe, from Scandinavia for example, were especially likely to go abroad for their education even after the foundation of universities in their own countries. This *peregrinatio academica,* as it was called at the time, despite its difficulties and dangers, was simpler in one way at least than it is today, since lectures all over Europe were given in the same language: Latin.[11] Frankfurt in the sixteenth century was an intellectual metropolis of another kind, since it was the site of the only international European book fair until Leipzig founded a rival institution in the late seventeenth century.

[9]

Again, from a religious point of view, Rome was the metropolis of Europe in 1500, though its dominance would soon be challenged by Wittenberg and Geneva as the capitals of the Lutheran and Calvinist worlds respectively, centres of immigration for students and religious refugees, as well as centres of publication for books which spread the faith abroad. Rome was a major centre of information for European Catholics about the world beyond Europe, thanks to the reports which missionaries, especially the Jesuits, sent to their headquarters there. The city was also a major centre of information about Christianity for the inhabitants of Asia and Africa, thanks to the catechisms and Bibles, translated into many languages, from Syriac to Ethiopian, which were printed in Rome in the sixteenth and seventeenth centuries to help missionaries in their work.

In religion, Europe was of course becoming less centralized in the early modern period, despite the efforts of ecumenical christians to reunite the churches which had split at the Reformation. To the schism between western Christians and the Greek and Russian Orthodox was added the still deeper division between Catholics and Protestants, themselves rapidly subdivided into Lutherans, Calvinists, Zwinglians, Anabaptists, and others.

In the arts, on the other hand, the continent of Europe was becoming more centralized and more unified, as a result of the invention of printing and also, perhaps, of the gradual commercialization of culture, a rise of the market of which printing formed only a part. Partly as a result of these economic changes, a handful of European cities of the period may be regarded as leading centres for the collection and exchange of information about the whole world. Besides Rome, discussed above, they included Venice, Amsterdam, Paris and London.

Sixteenth-century Venice, for example, was in a privileged position for the collection of information about the Ottoman Empire, because the city had a permanent representative, the *bailo,* in Istanbul, officially there to look after the interests of the merchant community but also transmitting economic, political and even military news, which the Venetians relayed to the rest of Europe. Seventeenth-century Amsterdam performed a similar function, collecting information about the East and West Indies via the representatives of the East and West India companies in those parts and transmitting it to other European countries. The famous Amsterdam Stock Exchange was, among other things a major centre for the distribution of news, true and false (for it was not unknown for speculators to spread false rumours in order to push the price of stock up or down).[12]

A relatively short essay such as this one cannot usefully consider all the many forms taken by culture as well as all the major cities of Europe over two centuries. Three kinds of activity have therefore been selected for relatively detailed investigation in the hope that they may be used as cultural thermometers or measuring-rods. All three of these activities, arts or trades were generally located in major cities, and all three underwent both major changes and geographical displacements in the sixteenth and seventeenth centuries. The activities chosen might be described as the "3 Ps", in other words painting, performance, and printing. The aim will be to locate the most important centres of each art, and to determine the importance of Antwerp in each one, relative to other European (and finally, in the last section, extra-European) cities.

In a now famous essay, first published in the 1950s, two American anthropologists distinguished two cultural roles for cities. In the first place, what they called the "orthogenetic role", in other words "to carry forward, develop, elaborate a long-established local culture", as in the case of the sacred city of Benares and its role in the elaboration of Hindu tradition. In the second place, there is the "heterogenetic role", that of generating heresies and creating original modes of thought or "new states of mind", a role generally played by cosmopolitan, metropolitan cities (Vienna in the late nineteenth century, for instance), and encouraged by the interaction of people of "diverse cultural origins".[13]

However, the concept of a cultural metropolis surely includes more than the idea of a centre of production and even that of a centre of innovation. A centre implies a periphery- the two concepts are interdependent. To call a city a cultural metropolis implies that its artists – writers, actors, printers, and so on – influence the world outside, whether by travelling abroad themselves, by exporting their products, or by attracting outsiders to the city, whether they come as students or consumers of the arts. Indeed, the innovatory role of cities would be virtually impossible to sustain if it were not for these outsiders, who come because they hope to receive inspiration from the urban culture but often end by contributing to it and helping it to change and so to survive. Both emigrants and immigrants will therefore play a considerable role in this essay.

# Centres of Painting

The model of "centres and peripheries" has not been employed very often by art historians until now, but it has its uses in this domain.[14] Let us look at the cities of the early modern Europe with the best claims to be centres of the visual arts in general and of painting in particular: Florence, Venice, Rome, Antwerp, Amsterdam and Paris.

Although Florence in 1500 was no longer quite the city it had been in the fifteenth century, and its population was only 60,000 or thereabouts, it is the obvious city with which to begin so far as the visual arts are concerned. It was still the city of Botticelli (who had ten years more to live). Leonardo da Vinci returned in 1500, Michelangelo in 1501. Florence was a craft-industrial city with a relatively large number of artist's workshops. 84 workshops for wood-carving were recorded in the late 1470s, 54 for stonework and 44 for metalwork, while there were at least 30 figure painters practising in 1472.[15]

The city was also heir to what might be called a truly remarkable tradition of innovation and experiment in the arts, already outstanding in the age of Giotto, in other words the generation before the great plague of 1348-9. In the early fifteenth century, the great trio of Brunelleschi, Donatello and Masaccio were responsible for a number of remarkable creative experiments (to say nothing of their rivals, such as

Ghiberti and Masolino). In the late fifteenth century, Verrocchio and Botticelli were among the outstanding artists of Florence, but they had to face competition from the Pollaiuolo brothers, not to mention Verrocchio's pupil the young Leonardo.

This Florentine "tradition of the new" may well have been weakening in the sixteenth century, but as long as Michelangelo was alive – and he lived until 1564 – it could hardly be said to be dead. The foundation of the famous Academy of Design in Florence, by Giorgio Vasari, had taken place in the previous year, to teach students as well as to raise the status of artists, and it did much to codify the distinctive characteristics of the Florentine tradition, notably the stress on draughtsmanship (*disegno*) at the expense of colour, on which the Venetian artists placed more emphasis.

Florence was also a major cultural centre in the sense that its artists and their products were in great demand abroad and that foreigners came to the city to learn how to emulate them. Like Florentine cloth, Florentine painting was well known in other parts of Europe.

Princes and patricians of the sixteenth century, in Italy and elsewhere, from Isabella d'Este in Mantua to Rudolf II in Prague, were beginning to collect paintings and sculptures and to treat them as "works of art", in other words as interesting and valuable not so much on account of their subject-matter or their material, or even their rarity, as on account of the artist who made them. What the collectors were increasingly interested in acquiring was not so much "a Madonna", for example, as "a Leonardo". In order to furnish the collectors with what they were looking for, a new occupation came into existence, that of art dealer. One of the first known in Europe is Gianbattista Della Palla, a Florentine patrician who bought and sold works by Florentine masters, especially to the court of France in the age of

Francis I. The rise of this international art market is one illustration of what was decribed above as the commercialization of culture.[16]

Florentine artists as well as their works were in increasing demand abroad. Leonardo spent the last years of the fifteenth century at the court of the Sforzas in Milan. After a few years in Florence he left again for France, where he served kings Louis XII and Francis I. The Florentine painters Jacopo Pontormo and Giovanni Battista Rosso, like the goldsmith Benvenuto Cellini, all worked for the king of France. In fact, however, none of these men, apart from Rosso were Florentines in the strict sense of the term. Leonardo came from the village of Vinci, in Tuscany, Michelangelo from Caprese, and Pontormo from the village of Pontormo, also in Tuscany. They went to Florence to study precisely because it was an artistic metropolis, while the immigration of such gifted young men made Florence even more metropolitan.

All the same, these self-perpetuating mechanisms are rarely effective for more than a few generations. By 1500, Venice, with more than 150,00 inhabitants, could reasonably challenge Florence's claim to be the centre of the arts, at least in painting. The Bellini brothers, Carpaccio, and Giorgione were all active, while the young Titian entered Giovanni Bellini's workshop at about this time. It is more difficult to estimate the total number of artists in Venice than it is for Florence, but the figures were roughly comparable. In 1624, 306 heads of household were engaged in artistic activities (including glass-making).[17]

Some of these artists came to Venice from outside. Giorgione came from Castelfranco in north Italy, Titian from Pieve di Cadore. Carpaccio's name suggests his family was from the Carpathians. Albrecht Dürer visited Venice to see what was going on in the art world, and met Giovanni Bellini. Bellini was invited abroad by foreign patrons, his brother Gentile travelled as far afield as Istanbul (where he painted the sultan Mehmet II, "the Conqueror"), and another Venetian artist, Jacopo de' Barbari, settled in northern Europe. Paintings too were exported. There was already an art market in Venice, with professional dealers such as the Catalan Juan Ram. Venetian architects were in demand abroad, especially in central Europe, following the routes of Venetian trade with Nuremberg.[18]

By all our criteria, then, Venice was an artistic metropolis, and remained one till the end of the sixteenth century, or at least till the deaths of Veronese (a migrant from Verona) in 1588 and of Tintoretto (a native son) in 1594.

Even in the seventeenth century, when there were no major painters active in the city, and the style of the minor painters was becoming increasingly provincial, Venice remained a goal of cultural pilgrimage, so much so that the profession of *cicerone* or guide came into existence in order to profit from the desire of visitors to be shown the cultural glories of the past. The faking of old masters was not unknown, the paintings being exposed to smoke to make them look older than they were. One of the leading art dealers in Europe in the early seventeenth century, the Netherlander Daniel Nys, ran his international business from a palazzo in Venice, selling paintings by Titian, Tintoretto, Veronese and so on to English nobles and also to King Charles I. The city was also one of the first places in Europe where paintings were exhibited in public.[19]

Rome, despite its relatively low population of 50,000 in the mid-sixteenth century, was another obvious competitor for the title of artistic metropolis, especially at the time of the so-called "High Renaissance" of the early sixteenth century. Few artists were born in Rome (Giulio Romano is one of the rare exceptions to this rule), but the papal court was a great centre of consumption and patronage, and so a magnet which attracted artists from all over Italy and sometimes from beyond. Michelangelo had already lived in Rome before 1500, and he returned there in 1505 to work on the pope's tomb and the ceiling of the Sistine Chapel. In the age of Julius II and Leo X, magnificent patrons both, Bramante and Raphael would arrive from Urbino, Baldassare Peruzzi from Siena, Polidoro from Caravaggio, Giovanni da Udine from Udine, and so on. In 1534, the guild of painters (which here included embroiderers) had no fewer than 220 practitioners on its books, and this was after the notorious sack of Rome by imperial troops in 1527, which had led to an exodus of artists.[20]

The artistic importance of the city did not end with the sack of 1527. It was revived in the later sixteenth century, thanks to the patronage of cardinal Farnese in particular, and it continued at least until the age of Bernini (1598-1680), which was also the age of art-loving popes such as Urban VIII and Alexander VII, cardinals such as Scipione Borghese, and other churchmen such as Cassiano del Pozzo (best-known for his interest in Poussin). Artistic production was also stimulated by the foreign visitors who generally came to see the classical antiquities but often departed with paintings by Guercino, Domenichino or Salvator Rosa (all three artists immigrants to Rome, the first two from Bologna and the last from Naples). Rome was carrying on its tradition of being a consumer rather than a producer of artists. The painter Michelangelo Merisi da Caravaggio came to the city from Lombardy, the architect Francesco Borromini from Milan, while Bernini came from Naples (his father, also an artist, having been attracted by the prospect of working for pope Paul V).

The Frenchmen Claude Lorraine and Nicolas Poussin were other artist-immigrants to a city which by 1600 had passed the 100,000 mark. Jan Asselijn, who was born in Dieppe, was another. There was also a colony of artists from the Netherlands, including two Antwerpers, Paul Brill and Jan Miel, and a number of Dutchmen, such as Bartolomeus Breenbergh and the brothers Pieter and Roeland van Laer. Like Venice, Rome was an early centre of art exhibitions. Again like Venice, it was an early centre of faking. Giulio Mancini, physician and dilettante, wrote a book on connoisseurship which explained how fake old masters were painted on genuine old panels, and gave his readers practical advice on methods for distinguishing genuine works from forged ones. Rome was also an international training centre for artists, a training which took institutionalized form with the foundation of the Accademia di San Luca in 1593 and of the Académie française de Rome in 1666.[21]

Thus Florence, Venice and Rome were all centres for the patronage and training of artists, for collecting and connoisseurship, and for the production, sale, forging, and history of works of art (activities which have often been associated, from Europe to China, as Joseph Alsop has argued in his comparative study of the "rare art traditions").[22] Fakes of ancient statues and medals were produced in the sixteenth century, and fakes of modern painters in the seventeenth century, all this on a sufficient scale to encourage experts to explain to collectors how the fakes might be detected. As for the history of art, it was born, or reborn, in Renaissance Florence, where Giorgio Vasari published his famous *Lives* of painters, sculptors and architects in 1550, a book which was taken as a model by Carlo Ridolfi in his lives of Venetian artists, and by Gian Pietro Bellori and Gian Battista Passari in their lives of the artists of Rome.

In all these respects the three Italian cities had few or no rivals elsewhere in Europe in the sixteenth century. Although Paris, for example, was already a major city, which held about 150,000 people in 1500 and doubled its size by 1565, it was not a major artistic centre in the sixteenth century, despite the proximity of the court. In any case, the court was not fixed in Paris, in the Louvre, but moved from one royal palace to another, from Blois to Chambord, from Chambord to Fontainebleau, and so on. The so-called "School of Fontainebleau" was a small group of artists, mainly Tuscans, in the service of King François I, who decorated the famous gallery in the palace.

Nuremberg, on the other hand, was an artistic centre, the home not only of Dürer but also of his followers the Beham brothers and of his pupil Hans Baldung (who came from Strasbourg), as well as famous sculptors, but it was only a medium-size town with about 20,000 inhabitants.[23] Prague was an artistic centre for a brief period at the end of the sixteenth century thanks to the patronage of the emperor Rudolf II, who employed (among others) the Milanese painter Giuseppe Arcimboldo, Adrian de Vries, Hans von Aachen, and the Antwerper Bartholomaeus Spranger, but its importance lasted no longer than Rudolf's reign. A city of some 30,000 people could not sustain a metropolitan role without imperial patronage, and later emperors preferred to live in Vienna.[24]

The only city in Renaissance Europe which offered a home to artists on the scale of Florence, Rome and Venice was Antwerp, which pulled ahead of its rivals in the Netherlands, from Bruges to Brussels, in the early sixteenth century. Dürer visited Antwerp as he had visited Venice, and acquired a number of exotic objects there. Even if the Italian immigrant Lodovico Guicciardini was exaggerating when he wrote of three hundred artists at work in the city in 1560, the fact that a Florentine should have been impressed by their numbers is testimony in itself. As in the case of Florence and Venice, an art market developed at Antwerp, together with exhibitions of paintings (from 1540 onwards in a permanent gallery at the Bourse), an interest in antiques, in faking them and finally in the detection of the fakes.[25]

Antwerp's importance as an artistic centre naturally suffered during the Revolt of the Netherlands. The great wave of iconoclasm of 1566 hit Antwerp cathedral particularly hard. The Spanish Fury of 1576, when the troops ran amok, also damaged works of art, while the migration of Protestant artists following Parma's capture of the city in 1585 made it more difficult to replace what had been destroyed.[26] All the same, Antwerp did manage to recover its position and to replace its artistic patrimony by the early seventeenth century, a time of some munificent patrons such as Cornelis van der Geest, whose fine art collection was painted by Willem van Haecht.[27] Indeed, the city rose to new heights in the age of Rubens and remained important as a "nurse of painters" – to quote the title of the famous image by Bueyermans, – for some years after his death. In 1663, for example, David Teniers II founded an academy of art at Antwerp on the model of the earlier academies of Florence, Rome and Paris.

By this time, Antwerp had northern rivals. In 1585, Amsterdam was still a provincial town with a population of around 30,000 and it was not famed for its artists. However, the flood of emigrants from the southern Netherlands who arrived in Amsterdam in the late sixteenth century included a number of painters and their families, such as Hans Bol and David Vinckboons from Mechelen, Roelant Savery from Kortrijk, and Gillis van Coninxloo, Paul Vredeman de Vries and Willem and Adriaen van Nieulandt from Antwerp.

By the late seventeenth century, Amsterdam had become a major city of some 200,000 inhabitants, and from the artistic point of view it was associated with the recent achievements of Rembrandt, Bartholomeus van der Helst, Ferdinand Bol, Govaert Flink, and many others. Indeed, there were probably some three hundred master painters at work in the city by this time. If Antwerp was the home of major art patrons such as the spice merchant Cornelius van der Gheest and the patrician Nicholas Rockox, Amsterdam had burgomaster Jan Six, the physician Nicolaes Tulp and the armaments magnate Louis Trip (all three men were patrons of Rembrandt, as well as of many other painters).[28]

The art market, which became increasingly large in the 1630s and 1640s, was probably even more important (from the economic point of view, at least) than patrician patronage. Inventories of the stock of no fewer than seven art dealers in seventeenth-century Amsterdam have been discovered, the largest enterprise being that of Johannes Renialme, who in 1657 was the owner of 565 paintings worth on average 64 guilders apiece, and including some old Italian masters.[29] Paintings were also sold at fairs and an English visitor to Amsterdam in 1640, Peter Mundy, was surprised to learn that butchers and bakers, blacksmiths and cobblers all bought paintings to decorate their homes, a feature of Dutch culture which has been confirmed by recent research.[30]

As in Florence, Venice and Rome, an interest in art history developed alongside an interest in collecting and dealing. Carel van Mander, the so-called "Dutch Vasari", published his *Schilderboeck,* or lives of the painters, in 1604, the year after he had settled in Amsterdam, while Arnold Houbraken, a Dordrecht man who also moved to Amsterdam, published his collection of artist's lives there in 1718-21 under the title *De Groote Schouburgh der Nederlandsche Konstschilders en Schilderessen.*

In the late seventeenth century, the distinctiveness of the painting of Amsterdam, like that of the Dutch republic, declined, and artists increasingly followed French models. It was at last the turn of Paris to become what it was long to remain, one of the great artistic centres of the western world. The rise of Paris was in part the result of the efforts of the king himself, of his minister Jean-Baptiste Colbert and of Colbert's adviser on artistic matters, Charles Lebrun, director of the art "factory" at the Gobelins, and head of the Academy of Painting. The foundation of the French Academy in Rome for the training of young artists was in a sense an admission of French inferiority or provincialism, but it was also an attempt to escape from this position, to learn from the Italians in order to surpass them.

Foreign artists had made their way to Paris in earlier generations. Philippe de Champaigne, for example, who came from Brussels, settled in Paris in 1628. However, from the beginning of the so-called "personal rule" of the young Louis XIV in 1661, the scale of state patronage was such as to entice artists to Paris in greater numbers than before. Gérard Edelinck, who made a number of portraits of Louis, came from Antwerp, and Adam-Frans de Meulen, who became one of Louis XIV's favourite war artists, came from Brussels. Bernini visited Paris, on loan to Louis from the pope. From the French provinces came the painters Hyacinthe Rigaud (from Perpignan), Jean Jouvenet (from Rouen), and many more, while the sculptors attracted to Paris included Antoine Coysevox from Lyon, Martin Desjardins (originally van den Bogaert) from Breda, François Girardon from Troyes, and Pierre Puget from Marseille. A number of artists were given lodgings and studios in the royal palace of the Louvre, which Louis XIV had deserted in favour of Versailles. At the end of the reign, public exhibitions of paintings were being organized at the Louvre.

It was only a generation later, however, from the year 1737, that these exhibitions, known as *salons,* became regular events, taking place every two years (like the Biennale in

Venice in our own time), mainly in the month of September. These exhibitions encouraged the rise of art criticism, notably Diderot's *Salons* in the 1760s, annual reviews of new paintings (on the model of the book reviews in learned journals, or the reviews of new plays), which did much to spread the knowledge of new developments abroad and thus make Paris the cultural centre of a wider area.[31] It will be no surprise to discover that both an art market and art history could also be found in Paris at this time. Edme-François Gersaint, for example, was a leading art dealer in the early eighteenth century as well as a friend of Watteau, who immortalized the contents of Gersaint's shop in the famous shop-sign he painted in 1721. In the course of compiling catalogues of the art collections he sold, Gersaint became involved in art history, and ended up making a catalogue raisonné of the work of Rembrandt. Pierre-Jean Mariette, best known for his lives of French artists (still an indispensable source) came of a family of art dealers.[32]

As a centre for painters, London lagged far behind Paris. A few foreign painters who went to London in the hope of making a reputation were not disappointed, but the reason for their success may well have been the lack of native competition. Hans Holbein, for example, who painted portraits of leading figures of the court of Henry VIII; Anthony van Dyck, who painted the court of Charles I; Peter Lely, who painted the court beauties of the age of Charles II: and Godfrey Kneller, who arrived in London in the mid-1670s and remained for nearly fifty years, living in a fashionable house in Covent Garden and painting fashionable portraits.

Only from the end of the seventeenth century onwards are there signs that artists were attracted to London by the presence of other artists. It was at that time that the young James Thornhill came to London from Dorset, in order to study with Thomas Highmore, painter to the court. In

1711, the first academy for the training of artists was founded in London, in Lincoln's Inn Fields, with Kneller as its first director. In the early 1730s, the young Allan Ramsay arrived from Edinburgh, to study at the academy in St Martin's Lane. Joshua Reynolds came from Devonshire to London in 1740, to be apprenticed to the portrait-painter Thomas Hudson, while his great rival Thomas Gainsborough arrived a couple of years later, from Suffolk, to study in St Martin's academy.

Hogarth, a native-born Londoner, followed another artistic trajectory, since he began as an engraver and book-illustrator in a city with a long tradition as a printing centre (see p. 50). Another London-born engraver, George Vertue, spent much of his spare time in the study of the history of English art. The gentleman-dilettante Horace Walpole bought Vertue's notebooks from his widow and transformed them into his *Anecdotes of Painting* (1762-71). In this case too we can see connexions between the rise of art history and the rise of new artistic institutions (if not an art market).

For the 1760s mark a turning-point in the history of London as a centre of art, or at least as a centre of painting. 1760 was the year of the first public exhibition in London of the work of British artists, an exhibition which took place in the Strand at the premises of the newly-founded Society of Arts. The Society offered annual prizes for paintings, and this institution acted as a magnet for artists. George Romney, for instance, came to London from Lancashire in 1762, after he was already a reasonably well-known portrait-painter in the North of England, in order to participate in the competition, and remained in the capital thereafter. In 1768, the Royal Academy was founded, following the Italian and French models, as at once a school for artists, a setting for exhibitions of their work, and finally a symbol of their rising status, appropriately embodied by their dignified and articulate first president, Joshua Reynolds, now Sir Joshua. London had become a metropolis for what some critics consider the peculiarly British genre of portrait-painting.

# Centres of Performance

The centres of most of the great European cities of the early modern period were stages for many kinds of drama; religious and secular, official and unofficial, indoor and outdoor, formal and informal, permanent or occasional.

In Florence, for instance, the great day of the ritual year was the feast of the city's main patron, St John the Baptist, in late June, *la festa di San Giovanni,* which included pageants (with floats representing the birth of San Giovanni, his baptism of Christ and so on). The festival included secular elements of a kind to be found in many parts of Europe at this time, such as a giant and a giantess, men walking on stilts, races, bull-baiting, and bonfires (perhaps a vestige of a pagan Midsummer festival which the Church had incorporated into its calendar).

A more unusual feature of the festival in its Florentine form was the ritualised presentation of tribute to San Giovanni by deputations coming from the Tuscan cities under Florentine domination, such as Pisa, Arezzo, Volterra, Cortona, and so on. It seems reasonable to suggest that the saint was seen as a personification of the city he protected, and even that this ritual was essentially a celebration of the dignity and power of Florence itself.[33]

In the carnival of Florence, the central element was a procession through the streets with many floats (the model

[27]

which is followed to this day, though on a much grander scale, by the famous *desfile* of the *escolas de samba* in the carnival of Rio de Janeiro). Another characteristic element in the Florentine carnival was the football match played on piazza Santa Croce by young Florentine patricians, at least in the seventeenth century. Whether or not football should be regarded as a form of ritual, it is difficult to deny that in this particular case the game was highly ritualised, beginning with formal challenges reminiscent of a medieval tournament.

In Venice, the election of doges and other high dignitaries was marked by processions and by the throwing of money to the crowd. The doge was also crowned, shown to the people in the church of San Marco, and carried round the piazza by the *arsenalotti,* the workers in the Venetian Arsenal, a kind of state-organized factory for the construction of ships. The doge's funeral rites included a procession to piazza San Marco and then to the church of Saints Giovanni e Paolo. Again, in Venice the festival of Corpus Christi was as much a civic as a religious festival. It was celebrated by pageants as well as by a procession to the sound of music around piazza San Marco. The feasts of San Marco, San Giorgio, San Sidro, San Stefano, San Vidal and San Rocco, Easter, Ascension, Palm Sunday and the feast of All Saints took similar forms.[34]

In Venice, even Carnival included an element of civic ritual – the solemn execution of twelve pigs and a bull on the Piazzetta, in the presence of the doge, the senators and foreign ambassadors. The animals were provided by the province of Friuli, which was part of the Venetian empire, as a form of tribute, like the gifts made to Florence by its subject cities on the feast of St John. Foreigners were already observing these rituals in the fifteenth century, and the size of the foreign audience for the Carnival of Venice, like the Carnival of Rome, increased over the years.[35]

Venice was also the scene of many "extraordinary" (in other words, non-recurrent) public rituals. In 1468-9, for example, there was the state entry of the emperor Frederick III. In 1499, the celebration in piazza San Marco of a naval victory over the Ottoman Empire and also a procession celebrating the League of Blois. In 1526, a procession in honour of the League of Cognac. In 1571, a procession in piazza San Marco in honour of the Holy League, which was followed by four days of celebrations for the victory of Lepanto. In 1573, the state visit of Henri III of France, on his way back from Poland to claim his kingdom. In 1579, there was a procession to beg for an end to the rain. In 1585, a procession in honour of the arrival of the Japanese envoys.

Most major European cities were the scene of festivals of this kind, though rarely as frequently or with the same magnificence as Venice. Royal entries into cities such as Paris and London, like the *possesso,* in other words the ritual by which the newly-elected pope took "possession" of the city of Rome, were all occasions of public rejoicing on which triumphal arches were erected in the streets, the facades of private houses were decorated, the fountains ran with wine, and both amateur and professional actors made speeches of welcome to the prince.

For a concrete example of such festivals, we might examine the entry of the emperor Charles V into London in June 1522. The civic authorities informed the Italian and Hansard merchant communities of the planned entry and requested contributions towards the pageants. The London city companies provided the rest of the money. Henry VIII and Charles V entered London in procession and were met by the mayor and aldermen together with the humanist Sir Thomas More, who made a speech in Latin. On London

Bridge the princes saw the figures of two giants, Hercules and Samson, and also Medea and Jason (in honour of the Order of the Golden Fleece of which Charles was the head). In Gracechurch Street, the Hanseatic merchants had built three towers, each representing a scene in the life of Charles's predecessor Charlemagne. In Leadenhall Street, the Italian merchants had built a genealogical tree, exhibiting the common ancestry of Charles and Henry, while in Cornhill King Arthur was represented sitting at his famous Round Table.[36]

Public festivals of this kind changed gradually over time. In Protestant cities, the traditional religious festivals were generally abolished, thus giving greater salience to the political festivals which survived and indeed often became more magnificent. In London, for example, the major event of the ceremonial year was now the Lord Mayor's Show. In this ritual of inauguration, the newly-elected Lord Mayor of London went in procession through the city and viewed floats designed in his honour, that of the "company" (in other words, guild), to which he belonged, and that of the city as a whole. This secular ritual might be interpreted as a secular equivalent of, or compensation for, the feast of Corpus Christi, which had been popular in England as elsewhere in late medieval Europe, and took place at much the same time of year as the Show, in early summer.[37]

The sixteenth century marks even more of a turning-point in the history of European drama. At the beginning of the century, as in the late Middle Ages, the majority of plays were religious and these plays were generally performed in temporary settings, often out of doors, in the market-place, and only on the occasion of major festivals such as Carnival, Easter, Corpus Christi or the feast of St John the Baptist. The actors were generally amateurs, members of a guild or confraternity (or in the Netherlands, a chamber of rhetoric).[38] In Paris, religious plays were performed from 1402 onwards by the Confrérie de la Passion. In England, the "mystery plays", as they were called, were staged in the streets by the guilds of leading towns such as York and Chester. Alternatively, religious plays might be performed in churches. In Florence, for instance, *rappresentazioni sacre,* like Feo Belcari's *Abraham and Isaac,* were performed in churches such as Santo Spirito or the Carmine.[39]

As for the relatively few secular plays of the fifteenth and early sixteenth centuries, they were generally performed in private houses, to celebrate weddings or seasonal festivals like Christmas and Carnival. In Florence, for example, Machiavelli's comedy *Mandragola* was first performed in a private house around the year 1520, by which time it was common for comedies to be played in the palaces of Venetian noble families such as the Contarini, the Foscari, or the Pesaro. Another important venue for secular plays in the early sixteenth century, as in the late Middle Ages, was the royal court. The comedies of the goldsmith-poet Gil Vicente, for instance, were regularly staged at the court of the king of Portugal.

In the later sixteenth century, however, we see a general rise of secular plays, performed for the general public on payment of a fairly modest fee by professional actors in permanent settings, often purpose-built playhouses situated in major European cities. It is likely that the growth of cities beyond a certain threshold was needed in order to make such permanent play-houses economic propositions, allowing a company to present the same play for several days or weeks outside the festive season and still find audiences, thus giving the actors a return on their investment in learning their lines without compelling them to spend their lives on the road. The rise of the commercial theatre at much the same time in a number of different parts of Europe suggests that what might be called the "critical mass" of population necessary for this development was about 100,000 people. Since some of the profit came from the sale of more expensive seats, the conditions favouring the rise of the commercial theatre included the presence of a wealthy group of citizens or nobles as well as that of journeymen artisans or apprentices to fill the cheaper places.[40]

In Seville, for example, plays were staged in orchards in the late sixteenth century, and in permanent theatres, notably the Coliseo, in the early 1600s. In Genoa, a permanent theatre was constructed in 1575 (though this one was not open to the general public). In Naples, the first permanent theatre, the Stanza della commedia di San Giorgio de' Genovesi, opened in 1592, to be followed by three competitors in the early seventeenth century. In Venice, which had had a public theatre as early as 1508, the real rise of the commercial drama took place in the seventeenth century. The Teatro di San Cassiano opened its doors in 1637, but by the end of the century no fewer than seven theatres were functioning, with operas dominating their repertoire. The rise of the theatres was doubtless encouraged by the rise of tourism (in the sense of participation in the "Grand Tour" by European aristocrats to finish off their education). However, the theatres also attracted an audience from a broad section of the local population, from the gondoliers standing in the pit to the patrician families who often owned their own boxes and came every night, as much to eat, drink, talk, flirt, see and be seen by the rest of the audience as to watch (let alone listen to) the performance.[41]

Three more cities in which the rise of the theatre was a spectacular event were Madrid, London and Paris. Madrid, for example, grew rapidly after it was made the seat of the court in 1561 (to reach 70,000 or even 100,000 inhabitants in the mid-seventeenth century). At the same time and for the same reason, the city became a centre of conspicuous consumption. At first plays, which were sponsored by confraternities in order to raise money for the hospitals under their care, were staged in yards [*corrales*], often attached to inns. Some of the audience sat on benches, while an awning protected them from the sun. However, these informal and possibly uncomfortable conditions for playgoing did not last for very long. The two major settings for plays, the Corral de la Cruz and the Corral del Príncipe, were soon converted into permanent theatres, complete with changing-rooms for the actors and boxes for the better-off members of the public. The prolific dramatist Lope de Vega was closely associated with these developments.[42]

In London, the rise of the public theatre took place at much the same time as in Madrid, and for similar reasons. The city was growing in the sixteenth century, and at the same time it too was becoming more of a centre for conspicuous consumption, as nobles and gentry began to build or to rent town houses and to spend at least a few months a year in the capital.[43] It was in 1576 that James Burbage erected the first permanent theatre in England at Shoreditch, in East London (and so outside the control of the City authorities, who viewed playhouses, like taverns, brothels and gaming houses, with considerable suspicion). He went on to convert a house in East London into a theatre, the Blackfriars. The London theatres of the end of the sixteenth century included the Fortune in Cripplegate, in East London, and the Rose, the Hope, the Swan and the Globe, all built on or near the bank of the Thames at Southwark, again in East London. The capacity of the Swan has been estimated at three thousand, that of the Fortune at more than two thousand. All in all, it is likely that around the year 1600 the London theatres attracted over 20,000 spectators a week, at a time when about 160,000 people lived within walking distance of them.

The annual repertoire of all the theatres combined was a considerable one. At least thirty-five plays are known to have been performed in London in the year 1600, and there may well have been some which have gone unrecorded, especially performances on the fringe of the theatrical world, like the puppet-plays at fairs (notably Bartholomew Fair in Smithfield every August). These public theatres were commercial enterprises – Shakespeare was one of the people with shares in the Globe – and the entry fee of a penny opened them to a substantial proportion of the urban population. Indeed, the master craftsmen and the municipal authorities were worried by the numbers of apprentices who frequented playhouses when they should have been working (plays were generally performed during working hours). However, it was not only the apprentices who went to see plays. Women formed a substantial part of the audience, and so did students from the Inns of Court (including the poet John Donne, described in his youth as "a great frequenter of plays"). On one occasion in 1602, when recruits for the army were needed, officers waited outside the theatres by order of the Privy Council in order to "press" (in other words, kidnap) members of the audience for compulsory military service. They probably shared the official stereotype of a theatre audience as composed for the most part of idle apprentices. Somewhat to their embarrassment, however, according to a contemporary news-letter, "they did not only press gentlemen and serving-men but lawyers, clerks, country men that had law causes, aye the Queen's men, knights, and as it was credibly reported, one earl".[44] This description is the nearest thing to a social survey of a seventeenth-century theatre audience which has survived. Worth noting is not only the lack of cultural and social homogeneity in the audience but the presence of visitors from the provinces.

Once begun, the London theatrical tradition lasted for a long time. Outlawed during the Puritan Revolution, plays and players returned to London with the restoration of the monarchy in 1660. Forty-seven plays are known to have been performed in London in 1662. The range of theatres may be illustrated from the career of Thomas Betterton, an actor-manager of the period, who was active at the Cockpit in Drury Lane, in Lincoln's Inn Fields, at Dorset Garden (on the bank of the Thames), at the Theatre Royal Drury Lane, which opened its doors in 1663, and at the Queen's Theatre in the Haymarket. By this time the population of the city had grown to little less than half a million.

A vivid description of the audience in a London theatre at the end of the seventeenth century was furnished by a foreign visitor, Henri Misson. "The pit is an amphitheatre, filled with benches without backboards, and adorned with green cloth. Men of quality, particularly the younger sort, some ladies of reputation and virtue, and abundance of damsels that hunt for prey, sit all together in this place, higgledy-piggledy, chatter, toy, play, hear, hear not. Farther up, against the wall, under the first gallery, and just opposite to the stage, rises another amphitheatre, which is taken up by persons of the best quality, among whom are generally very few men. The galleries, whereof there are only two rows, are filled with none but ordinary people, particularly the upper one". The mixture of classes is still apparent but the proportions seem to have changed. There are more ladies and gentlemen, and fewer apprentices visible than there were a hundred years earlier.

By the middle of the eighteenth century, the age of the great actor David Garrick, the London theatre scene was in a still more flourishing condition. At least 86 plays were staged in the 1746 season. Most of these plays could be seen in the three major theatres in Drury Lane (which could hold some two thousand spectators), Covent Garden, and Goodman's Fields (in Whitechapel, in East London), but others were performed in theatres on the fringe such as the Bowling Green. It has been calculated that two theatres alone, Drury Lane and Covent Garden, attracted some 22,000 spectators a week by 1762. London, which was still growing fast – to reach a total of something like 900,000 inhabitants by the end of the eighteenth century – was indeed a theatrical metropolis at this time.[45]

It may seem strange to have discussed London at such length without saying anything about Paris. The point is that the development of Paris as a theatre centre occurred relatively late. In 1548 the first permanent theatre in the city was built in rue Mauconseil on the ruins of a palace belonging to the Duke of Burgundy. The Hôtel de Bourgogne, as it was called, was owned by the Confrérie de la Passion, but as they were now forbidden to perform plays themselves they leased the building to professional actors. A second theatre was the Petit-Bourbon, constructed within the palace of the Dukes of Bourbon in 1577. Two theatres does not seem very much for a city as large as Paris (with some 200,000 inhabitants at this time), but the wars of religion, which raged from the early 1560s until the early 1590s, may well have been the reason for this retarded development.

In the seventeenth century, however, four more theatres came into use, finally making the capital a metropolis of the drama. The first was cardinal Richelieu's theatre at the Palais-Royal. Originally private, the theatre became public when it was given to Molière in 1660, and after his death in 1673 to Jean-Baptiste Lully, who staged his operas there. The second was the Théâtre du Marais, a converted tennis-court in rue Vielle-du-Temple which opened its doors in

1634 and was abandoned in 1680. The third and fourth theatres, one in the rue Mazarine (the Hôtel de Guénégaud, another converted tennis court) and the other at the Étoile, were used by the Comédie française after their foundation in 1680, the year in which the Hôtel de Bourgogne was given to the Italian actors who played the *commedia dell'arte*.[46] The theatre continued to flourish in the eighteenth century just as the city continued to grow (by the time of the French Revolution it accommodated some 700, 000 people).

In the Netherlands the late medieval tradition of the amateurs organized in chambers of rhetoric continued to flourish in the early modern period. One might try to explain this rather unusual survival by saying that in literature (unlike humanism), the Renaissance came relatively late to the Netherlands, or alternatively, by pointing to the survival of other forms of civic consciousness in this region in an age in which European cities were generally losing power to the centralized state. After all, the defence of civic liberties was a major reason for the revolt of the Netherlands against Philip II.

In any case, the tradition of the chambers of rhetoric proved itself capable of being adapted to the purposes of religious controversy during the Reformation, and it remained vital throughout the sixteenth century. Antwerp had its Violiere, its Goudbloem and its Olijftak, while Amsterdam had De Eglantier, Het Wit Lavendel and Het Vijgeboomken (the last two chambers being new ones dominated by emigrants from the south).[47]

The members of De Eglantier included the poet Roemer Visscher; Pieter Cornelisz Hooft (the son of burgomaster Cornelis Pietersz Hooft) who was active as both a playwright and a historian; Gerbrand Adriaensz Bredero, the author of the famous comedy *The Spanish Brabanter;* and the professional physician and amateur playwright Samuel Coster, who broke with the chamber in 1617 (together with Bredero and Hooft) to found what was called the Nederduytsche Academie, an adaptation of the chamber of rhetoric to Renaissance forms of sociability on the Italian model. Coster was also behind the foundation of a public theatre in Amsterdam, the Schouwburg on the Keizersgracht, which was inaugurated in 1638, in other words the year after San Cassiano in Venice.[48] Among the plays to be seen there were those of Joost van den Vondel, who was born in Cologne, in 1587, whither his Mennonite parents had fled from Antwerp to escape religious persecution, but came to Amsterdam when he was still a child. Like other southerners, he joined Het Wit Lavendel rather than De Eglantier. Another leading playwright of the time was also an immigrant to Amsterdam and for similar reasons to Vondel's – Thomas Asselijn, whose family were Protestants from Dieppe who came to the Dutch Republic to escape the religious wars.

Antwerp did not follow the examples of Madrid, London, Paris or Amsterdam and set up a permanent public theatre. All the same, the absence of a playhouse of this kind in the sixteenth and seventeenth centuries did not mean that interest in the drama was lacking in the city. On the contrary, the Antwerpers Willem van Haecht (c1530-1612), of the Violiere, and Willem Ogier (1618-89), of the Olijftak, were famous, at least locally, for their plays. Performances took place in the traditional manner in public squares or in public buildings, belonging to the archery society, for example, the guild of St Luke, and so on.

The civic tradition of public festivals, religious and political, was also an extremely strong one in Antwerp. The *Ommegangs* were processions round the city in which all the major guilds and fraternities of the city took part, building floats on religious themes such as the Annunciation, the

Flight into Egypt, the Last Judgement and Hell, or secular themes such as the "Theatre of the World", shown in 1654, which represented the four known continents and thus symbolized the role of the city in international trade.[49] Like the chambers of rhetoric, these *Ommegangs* offer a dramatic example of the survival of a late medieval civic tradition into the early modern world.

Antwerp was also the scene of some magnificent "entries" by princes, including that of Charles V in 1520; that of prince Philip (later Philip II) in 1549; that of the Archdukes Albert and Isabella in 1599; that of the "Cardinal-Infante" Fernando, brother of King Philip IV and Governor of the Netherlands, in 1635. For Philip II's entry the decoration of the city was supervised by Pieter Coeck, for Fernando's by Rubens. In the latter case, the chamber of rhetoric known as the Goudbloem set up a stage near the town hall for a dramatic performance.[50]

The rise of musical performances followed similar lines in major cities after a time-lag of a century or so, suggesting that the proportion of the public with an appetite for concerts was a smaller one. Londoners seem to have been pioneers in this respect. The first recorded public concert took place in the Mitre Inn in London in 1664. A public concert room was opened near Charing Cross in 1678 and in the same year Thomas Britton began to organize a series of weekly concerts in Clerkenwell. By the eighteenth century, concerts were taking place in a number of London locales. The rise of concert-rooms was part of the general trend towards the "commercialization of leisure" and the "birth of a consumer society" discussed by historians such as J. H. Plumb, a trend which may be illustrated from such London-based performances as boxing-matches and circuses, which grew up in the eighteenth century alongside more traditional popular entertainments such as cock-fighting and bear-baiting. Thomas Topham, for example, gave public exhibitions of his strength in London in the 1730s and 1740s, lifting weights, bending iron pokers, and pulling against a horse. Jack Broughton, a pugilist turned impresario opened a boxing-ring in Oxford Street in 1743, charged for admission and advertised when matches would take place. Philip Astley, an equestrian performer, opened what we would now call a "circus" at Westminster Bridge in 1770, complete with jugglers, trapeze artists, wild animal trainers and so on.[51]

To coin a useful if clumsy term, we might speak of the increasing "metropolitanization" of English culture (both high and popular) at this time. There was a parallel trend in Paris, where André Philidor organized regular public concerts in the Tuileries from 1725 onwards, while the so-called "theatre of the fair" (an unofficial or fringe theatre including acrobats, marionettes, and exhibitions of freaks and mechanical devices) had its golden age in the years immediately before the French Revolution.[52]

# Centres of Printing

After the invention of printing with moveable type – whether or not the credit for the invention should go to Johann Gutenberg – in the middle of the fifteenth century, the new invention spread rapidly across Europe, carried by a diaspora of Germans in particular. By the year 1500, presses had been established in some 250 towns. Yet most books were printed in a relatively small number of cities.

So far as printing is concerned it may be possible to make a rough calculation of the relative importance of different cities on the basis of the number of printers at work before 1600 whose books may be found in the British Library (it cannot be shown that the books in the British Library are a random sample, but I know of no special reason why the collection should have been biassed in favour of a particular city). Fifty-nine of these printers were at work in Seville, for example, 64 in Salamanca and 65 in Barcelona. 76 were at work in Basel (among them such famous names as the Amerbach, Froben and Petri families, Oporinus and Perna). Seventy-nine were at work in Naples, and 84 in Florence (notably the Giunta family). A hundred and forty-five printers were at work in Antwerp, which was surpassed by only four cities. A hundred and ninety-five printers were at work in Rome (the best-known being Antonio Blado); 310 in Lyon (including Sebastian Gryphius and Guillaume Rouillé); 465 in Paris (including the Badius and Estienne families); and 660 in Venice.

The total number of printers at work in all these cities must have been considerably higher than the number of printers whose works are now in the British Library, but it may not be too imprudent to trust these figures as indicators of relative importance in the field of book production.[53] In all these cities, the printers included a substantial minority of immigrants (the Italian Perna in Basel, for instance), more especially Germans (the clerics Sweynheym and Pannartz in Rome, the Crombergers in Seville, Gryphius in Lyons, and so on).

Venice, long a centre of news, communication or "mediation" between east and west, the "hinge of Europe", as it has been called, had a particularly important role to play in the international book trade.[54] In the course of the fifteenth century, more books were printed in Venice than in any other city in Europe (4,500 editions and two and a half million copies seems a reasonable estimate). The press of Aldus Manutius, with 30 employees, has been described as "possibly the largest private industrial establishment in Venice". If the Florentines contributed more to the creation of the Renaissance, the Venetians surely contributed more to its diffusion, with the Aldine editions of the classics, such as the works of Plato in Greek, published in 1513, and the first edition of Castiglione's *Cortegiano* (1528).[55]

The work of Aldus Manutius was continued by such printers as Gabriel Giolito, who printed circa 850 books at Venice before his death in 1578. Giolito, incidentally, was the greatest printer of illustrated books of his time, and Venice was a major centre of print-making in the sixteenth century. Given its role as a centre of international trade, it is scarcely surprising to discover that map-making was another Venetian speciality in this period, or indeed that Venetian printers published many accounts of contemporary discoveries and explorations, whether in Asia or the Americas.

Renaissance Venice was more than a centre of printing. It was also a centre of writers, including some professional writers who were attracted to the city because printing was well-established there as well as for the freedom which Venice offered. The most famous of these writers was Pietro Aretino, a Tuscan who lived for a time in Rome but eventually settled in Venice because it offered him the best opportunities for making money from his pen without falling into dependence, like so many authors, on a single patron.

In the circle of Aretino – whether they were employees, friends, acquaintances or enemies – could be found a number of satellites, in other words minor writers with similar aims to his. Niccolò Franco, for instance, who came to Venice from Benevento, was Aretino's secretary. Ludovico Domenichi, who came from Piacenza, and Ludovico Dolce, who was born in Venice, both worked for the firm of Giolito. Girolamo Ruscelli, who came to Venice from Viterbo, worked for another printer, Valgrisi. Antonfrancesco Doni, who came from Florence, was himself active as a printer.

These men were known as the *poligrafi,* "the writers of many things", because they made their living by producing a large number of books on a considerable variety of subjects, whether they wrote them, edited them, compiled them, translated them or plagiarized them from books already in existence. It would be an exaggeration to say that the presence of these writers made Venice into a literary metropolis, but they do offer an unusually early example in European history of a group of young men with literary ambitions who are attracted by a great city. The dominance of Venice as a centre of printing and literature declined for two obvious reasons. In the first place, because of the spread of the Counter-Reformation and of the various organizations set up by the Church in order to fight the spread of heresy. The Inquisition was established in Venice in 1540 and a Venetian Index of Prohibited Books was produced in 1549. The booksellers of the city found themselves summoned before the tribunal and interrogated on charges of smuggling heretical books from abroad.[56] Printers were even more vulnerable than booksellers to ecclesiastical intervention of this kind. As a result, firms such as that of Gabriel Giolito found it prudent to shift their investments towards the publication of devotional books in Italian for a geographically more limited market. From the late sixteenth century onwards, Venetian printing and indeed Venetian culture as a whole, was becoming less metropolitan and more provincial. Hence it should not surprise us too much to discover a Venetian merchant, resident in Antwerp, writing home in 1563 that the city was one of "great liberty", despite the fact that this was the traditional claim made for Venice. His point was reinforced nearly twenty years later, when he had returned to Venice and was denounced to the Inquisition for the possession of prohibited books which he seems to have acquired in his Antwerp days.[57]

In the second place, the discovery of the new world inevitably undermined the importance of Venice as an information centre and commercial centre alike. In the short run the discoveries helped Venetian printers by offering them exciting new topics for books and pamphlets, but in the long run the shift in the centre of gravity of Europe westwards towards the Atlantic would inevitably weaken the position of Venice. It was therefore time for another city to take over the role of Europe's centre of information and communication.

For a period in the later part of the century, this role was shared by several different places. Lyons, for example, was a major printing centre in the middle of the sixteenth century, and might have kept its position longer if the French religious wars had not broken out in the 1560s. Some of the leading printers of Lyons were involved with the humanist movement, including Sebastian Gryphius (an emigrant from Germany who published over a thousand books in his city of adoption), or Guillaume de Rouillé, who married the daughter of an Italian colleague and himself published a number of works in Italian, including Castiglione's famous *Cortegiano*.[58] Again, it has been argued that the Protestant Reformation spread through Europe via books and pamphlets produced in three "frontier cities" in particular: Basel, Strasbourg, and Antwerp.[59] Basel was an academic city and a centre of humanism and so it is not surprising to find that its printers specialized in Latin works and in editions of the Bible. Strasbourg's printers, on the other hand, concentrated on works in the vernacular, and exploited the opportunities offered by their city's position on the border between the French-speaking and German-speaking worlds.[60]

Let us look at Antwerp printing in a little more detail. The city was a home to fifty-six printers between 1500 and 1540, nearly half of the printers at work in the whole Netherlands. With sixteen presses in 1574, and twenty-two in 1576, the firm headed by Christophe Plantin was one of the biggest in Europe, in the same class as the establishment of Aldo Manuzio in Venice.[61] As in the other great printing cities, the printers of Antwerp included a substantial proportion of foreign immigrants, among them Plantin himself, who came from France; Martin Lempereur, another Frenchman; "Gerard de Jode"; the Spaniard Francisco de Enzinas; and the German Arnoldus Mylius.[62] Appropriately enough for a centre of international trade, Antwerp was a major centre for printing maps and making globes, as the career of the scholar Abraham Ortelius reminds us.

In the early sixteenth century the city was also a refuge for heretics (including the Englishman William Tyndale and the Dane Christiern Pedersen), and a centre for the diffusion of their ideas. As a great international port, Antwerp offered unusual opportunities for communication between different parts of Europe, for those enterprising, daring, and polyglot enough to take advantage of them.

Martin Lempereur, for example, printed Protestant literature in French in Antwerp for export to France. Again, the New Testament in the vernacular versions of William Tyndale and Antonio Brucioli were published at Antwerp at a time when it was not safe to publish them in England or Italy. Book-burnings in the city in 1521 and 1522 were not sufficient to stop the production of unorthodox literature. It was a Catholic English merchant in Antwerp, Augustine Packington, who bought the whole edition of Tyndale in order to burn it on the instructions of the bishop of London (who seems not to have mastered the economics of printing).

According to a contemporary source, Edward Hall's *Chronicle,* "Augustine Packington came to William Tyndale and said, 'William, I know thou art a poor man, and hast a heap of new Testaments and books by thee for the which thou hast both endangered thy friends and beggared thyself, and I have now gotten thee a merchant which with ready money shall dispatch thee of all that thou hast, if you think it so profitable for your self.' 'Who is the merchant?' said Tyndale. 'The Bishop of London', said Packington. 'Oh that is because he will burn them', said Tyndale. 'Yea, Mary' quoth Packington. 'I am the gladder', said Tyndale, 'for these two benefits shall come thereof: I shall get money of him for these books to bring myself out of debt, and the whole world shall cry out upon the burning of God's word. And the overplus of the money that shall remain to me, shall make me more studious to correct the said New Testament, and so newly to imprint the same once again, and I trust the second will much better like you than ever did the first'. And so forward went the bargain, the Bishop had the books, Packington the thanks, and Tyndale had the money".[63]

This international city was an appropriate locale for publications in an international language. In fact, more than half the books printed in Antwerp between 1500 and 1540 were in Latin, including several works by Erasmus, from the *Adagia* to *De libero arbitrio*.[64] Among the Latin books first published there were at least twenty-six translations from the vernacular (usually Italian, Spanish or French).

In this polyglot city, with its communities of Italians, Portuguese, Spaniards, Jews, Germans, English and so on, it is no surprise to find that books were regularly produced in five modern languages (Flemish, French, English, Italian and Spanish), and even, occasionally, in Danish. Of one printer, Philippe Nutius, it was said that he "knew Latin, French, Spanish, Flemish, Italian and some German".[65] The Nutius family firm specialized in the printing of Spanish books (including Castiglione's *Cortegiano* in Spanish translation). Others printed Spanish literature – Guevara's *Reloj de príncipes*, for example, or the picaresque novel *Lazarillo de Tormes* – in French translations. Its polyglot environment made Antwerp an early centre for the production of newsletters and news-sheets (notably Abraham Verhoeven's *Tijdinge*, with their reports on the early stages of the Thirty Years' War).

Antwerp printers also published their share, or more than their share of books on the world outside Europe: López de Gómara on Mexico, Cieza de León on Peru, Damião Goes on Prester John, González de Mendoza on China, Lopes

[47]

de Castanheda and J. de Hese on India, Bartholomeus Georgevic's account of the Turks, a letter of the sultan Mehmed II, and so on. Among the translations into Latin first published in the city were the travels of Marco Polo and "Sir John Mandeville", a history of Peru by Torres Bollo, and a pioneering European account of the plants and herbs of the east Indies by the physician García de Orta.

The printing of images was an important part of the industry. The spread of Renaissance architecture and decorative motifs such as grotesques and "strapwork" throughout northern Europe would have been considerably slower had it not been for the pattern-books printed at Antwerp in the middle of the sixteenth century by Peter Coecke, Cornelis Floris, and Hans Vredeman de Vries.

The devotional engravings of the Wierix brothers had an international appeal, and indeed they exercised some influence on artistic conventions as far afield as India and China, where they were taken by Jesuit missionaries. Indeed, it has been argued that the illustrations by Anton Wierix to the 1579 edition of the *Theatrum Orbis Terrarum* of Abraham Ortelius made a considerable impact on Chinese landscape painting. Leading Chinese painters like Wu Pin did not exactly copy Wierix's images, but they seem to have been stimulated into innovation in response to them.[66]

If we measure it by new entries into the trade, Antwerp printing was at its most important between the 1540s and the early 1580s. After the city was recaptured by Parma, some printers left Antwerp (Niclaes Mollyns, for instance, Philippe Nuyts, or Gilles van den Rade, who established himself in Franeker), while others – like Gabriel Giolito in Venice – became less adventurous in their publications. Plantin is the obvious example of the trend. Before the siege he had published the Calvinist Philippe de Mornay's *Vérité de la religion chrétienne* and other "heretical" books, but afterwards he was careful not to offend the orthodox.

After 1585, Antwerp's printers, like those of Venice, came to specialize in the spread of the Counter-Reformation. One might say that they were saved from the provinciality of their Venetian colleagues by their role as middlemen between northern and southern Europe. Thus the city was the centre of the Catholic propaganda smuggled into England in the late sixteenth and early seventeenth centuries.[67] The city's printers also published many books by and about the Society of Jesus. For example, the *History of the Jesuits* by Nicolo Orlandino was published in Antwerp, by the heirs of Martin Nuyts, in 1620. A volume commemorating the canonization of Ignatius Loyola and Francis Xavier was published in the city in 1622. When the Jesuits celebrated the centenary of the foundation of the order in 1640, it was in Antwerp that this *Image of the First Century* was printed. When the Jesuit cardinal Sforza Pallavicino wrote a history of the Council of Trent defending it from the criticisms of Paolo Sarpi, an Antwerper published the work in Latin translation.

The translations from the vernacular into Latin printed in Antwerp in this period also included treatises on canon law, devotional works, and reports on Catholic missions in the East. Certain publishers in particular specialized in works associated with the Counter-Reformation, notably Plantin, Jan Mourentorf, who set up shop in the city in 1597 and went business with Plantin's widow, and Plantin's grandson and successor Balthasar Moretus. By 1600, Antwerp was also a centre for the publishing of popular literature in Flemish, notably romances of chivalry like the *Heemskinderen*.[68]

In the longer term, however, and in wider fields of publication, Antwerp did not remain competitive and leadership in the field of printing, and perhaps in that of communication more generally, passed elsewhere. One possible competitor, Lyons, suffered from the religious wars, as we have seen. London was another major printing centre, with a virtual monopoly of English printing. Like Venice in the middle of the sixteenth century, late sixteenth-century London attracted writers from the provinces, such as Robert Greene, who was born in Norwich, Thomas Nashe, who came from Lowestoft, Christopher Marlowe, who came from Canterbury, and of course the young man from Stratford-on-Avon. The opportunity to write for the theatre was one of the attractions, the existence of the Inns of Court (virtually a third university specializing in the study of law) was another, while a third was the massive presence of printers, publishers and booksellers in the city, centred on St Paul's Churchyard. Greene and Nashe, for example, published pamphlets, and Shakespeare narrative poems such as *Venus and Adonis*.

The role of London as a centre of men of letters, amateur and professional (the so-called "hack" writers) became even more important as the city grew in the course of the seventeenth and eighteenth centuries. The greatest concentration of professionals was in Grub Street in Cripplegate, defined by Dr Johnson in his famous Dictionary as "a street near Moorfields, much inhabited by writers of small histories, dictionaries and temporary poems". Hence the traditional English description of third-rate writers as "Grub Street hacks".

Third-rate writers were not of course the only ones to congregate in the city, whose cultural attractions now included clubs and coffee-houses as well as theatres and bookshops. Indeed, it might be argued that outstanding figures in any art are more likely to be found in locations and periods where there are large numbers of practitioners, whether painters in fifteenth-century Florence or playwrights in Elizabethan London. The age of Grub Street was also the age of Congreve and Dryden, Addison and Steele, Pope and Johnson, Fielding and Richardson.

Of these men only Alexander Pope was born in London. The playwright William Congreve was born in Yorkshire, came to London to study at the Middle Temple, but turned from law to literature. Edmund Burke also came to London, from Dublin in his case, to study at the Middle Temple, but turned to politics. The poet John Dryden came to London from Northamptonshire. Joseph Addison was born in Wiltshire and moved from Oxford to London when he was offered a minor political office, and then turned to journalism, together with his friend Richard Steele, who came from Dublin. Samuel Johnson was born in Lichfield, and left it in 1737 with his friend the actor David Garrick, both of them penniless, to try their fortunes in London. The novelist Samuel Richardson, who came from Derbyshire, went to London to become an apprentice, while Henry Fielding, who came from an upper-class family in Somerset, moved to the capital for social rather than economic reasons, like the Scotsman James Boswell, who recorded in his journal his excited reactions to the city. London was clearly a metropolis.

However, English was not a well-known language on the Continent until the later eighteenth century at the earliest, and London printers do not seem to have been prepared to publish in other languages on a grand scale (though one printer in Elizabethan London, John Wolfe, did publish both Machiavelli and Castiglione in Italian). London may have been a literary metropolis for the British Isles, but it did not perform this role for the Continent.

In a similar manner, Paris was becoming a literary metropolis for the rest of France. From the beginning of the seventeenth century, if not before, talented young men from the provinces made their way to the capital; Bossuet from Dijon, Corneille from Rouen, Malherbe from Caen, Pascal from Clermont-Ferrand, Racine from Soissons, Voiture from Amiens, and so on. They went to Paris to make their careers, attracted by the university, by the court, and by the theatres. To these attractions others were added in the course of the seventeenth century, notably the academies (the Académie française was founded in 1634), and the salons, of which the most famous was that of the Hôtel de Rambouillet, presided over by the marquise and her daughter. Paris, more exactly the court and the upper classes of the city (*la cour et la ville,* as the poet Boileau called it), was becoming the arbiter of literary taste.[69]

Since some 3,500 books were published in Paris in the decade 1551-60, it might have seemed that the city was ready to take over the role of Antwerp. However, development in this direction was hindered in Paris as in Lyons by the outbreak of the wars of religion in the later sixteenth century. The potential of Paris to become Europe's dominant centre of printing was also hindered as well as helped by the rise of absolute monarchy. On the one hand, the government was prepared to pay for prestige publications, and also journals such as the official *Gazette* (founded in 1631, and published from the Louvre), the *Journal des Savants,* an early example of the learned periodical (founded in 1665), and the *Mercure Galant* (founded 1672), perhaps the first women's magazine but also a journal which made propaganda for the regime and was later to be subsidized by the government).

On the other hand, censorship was strict. In the age of Louis XIV, his minister Colbert tried to concentrate Paris printing in a few hands so that it would be easier to control. In 1701 there were only 51 printing shops in Paris compared with 75 in 1644 and 181 in 1500. The official printers, such as Jean-Baptiste Coignard, did well out of the system, but the repertoire of the Paris printers as a whole was limited.

These obstacles in the way of potential rivals help to explain how it was that the international role of Antwerp passed to the boom town of Amsterdam, which grew from about 30,000 inhabitants at the beginning of the seventeenth century to 200,000 at its end (thanks in particular to the influx of Protestant refugees from the southern Netherlands). In seventeenth-century Amsterdam, printing was a leading industry, like brewing and soap-making. Indeed, between 1650 and 1700 Amsterdam was almost certainly the greatest centre in Europe for the production and marketing of books. The equivalent in the seventeenth century of the printing shops of Manutius and Plantin in the sixteenth was the establishment of the Blaeuw family on the Bloemgracht, which opened in 1637, and soon became one of the sights of Amsterdam, with its nine presses for printing text and six more for illustrations.[70] In the last quarter of the century, over 270 printers and booksellers were active in the city.[71]

Amsterdam's place as a metropolis of printing did not depend on the size of the book trade alone, but also on its orientation towards the export market. Like the Antwerpers, the Amsterdammers were polyglots. They printed books not only in Dutch and Latin but in French, Spanish, Italian, German, English, Hebrew, Hungarian, Swedish, and even Arabic, Armenian, Georgian and Yiddish, and did this so cheaply that they could outsell their local competitors from England to Lithuania. Some enterprising Amsterdam booksellers opened branches in other cities, as Jan Jansonius did in Frankfurt, Leipzig, Berlin, Danzig, Copenhagen and Stockholm.[72]

Other forms of printed matter were also important. The Dutch were great pamphleteers, as the famous collection in

The Hague shows.[73] Amsterdam has been described as "the earliest newspaper centre in Western Europe", producing news-sheets in Dutch, French, English and German.[74] In the second half of the seventeenth century, five newspapers in French alone were published in the city, including the *Nouvelles ordinaires* and the *Gazette d'Amsterdam,* often containing news which French journalists would not have been allowed to print. The Dutch were also the leaders in the field of map-making, with the Blaeuws in Amsterdam taking the place of Mercator in sixteenth-century Antwerp. Amsterdam was also a major centre for the production and marketing of prints, especially in the age of Romeyn de Hooghe, an Amsterdammer active as a writer and a graphic artist from the 1660s to the beginning of the eighteenth century. No wonder that the United Provinces in general and Amsterdam in particular have been described as a "centre of European information" at this time, as an "intellectual entrepôt", or as an "information exchange" which played a crucial role in the modernisation of capitalism.[75]

# Three Asian Cities

"Metropolis" is a rather grand term. If we are to justify the claim to that title on the part of certain European cities, the very least we can do is to try to place them in world perspective, comparing and contrasting them with certain cities outside Europe. Three obvious candidates for this kind of comparison in the early modern period are Istanbul, Peking and Edo (now Tokyo), all major cities in which the cultural life of the period has been described in some detail in studies available in western languages.

It is obviously perilous to approach non-western cultures with categories derived from western history, including the trio of painting, performance and print which is central to this essay. The great danger is that of characterizing other cultures in terms of what the west possessed and they lacked, at the same time forgetting or passing over the fact that these cultures might have possessed arts which the west lacked. All the same, the risks inherent in the process of comparison are surely worth running if it allows us to realize that what we call "the arts" were greatly valued in the great cities of the Middle and Far East, even if they were classified and organized in ways which differed from the western tradition.

Istanbul was one of the greatest of these cities, combining as it did the functions of a major international port with those of the court of the sultan and the capital of a great empire.[76] In the Ottoman Empire, despite Muhammed's famous statement that "All those who make an image go to hell", miniature painting flourished at court and illustrated the deeds of the ruler. The sultan Mehmed II, the conqueror of the Byzantine empire, was interested in western as well as in Ottoman art. He invited Gentile Bellini to Istanbul, and sent a Turkish painter, Sinan, to Venice. Both men painted the sultan's portrait. The sultan Murad III was another connoissseur of painted manuscripts.

All the same, Istanbul, like other cities in the Muslim world, lacked what might be called the public visual culture so important in western cities of this period – the statues in the squares, the paintings in the churches, the engravings in the shops, and so on. Miniature painting was an art of the private sphere, an art for an elite.[77]

In the case of print, too, the situation of Istanbul was very different from that of western cities of this period, for printed books were virtually non-existent. The American orientalist Marshall Hodgson has described the Ottoman, Safavid and Mogul states of this period as the "gunpowder empires".[78] It might be equally illuminating to call them the "manuscript empires". As in the medieval West, manuscript books were often beautifully written, and sometimes illustrated. Calligraphy was highly prized by collectors. The role of scribe (*warraq, nakkash*) was an honourable one, and sultan Beyazid himself did not disdain to practice it. Booksellers' quarters had a privileged location in the great bazaars in Istanbul as in other great Muslim cities. However, handicraft technology made books expensive. Only rulers (like the sultans) or wealthy private individuals (bureaucrats, for example) could afford to collect books on a large scale. Public libraries existed, attached to mosques, but they housed only religious books.

Islam has therefore been described with some accuracy as a barrier to printing as it spread slowly westward from China. The chequered history of the attempt to introduce printing in the Ottoman Empire reveals the strength of the obstacles to this form of communication. According to the imperial ambassador Ogier Ghiselin de Busbecq, writing in the middle of the sixteenth century, the Turks thought it a sin to print religious books. At the end of the century sultan Murad III allowed the sale of non-religious printed books in Arabic characters, but these were imported from Italy (where the first such book had been printed as early as 1514). The first Turkish press was established only in the eighteenth century, over two hundred years after the first Hebrew press in the Ottoman empire. It was founded on the initiative of Ibrahim Müteferriqa, a Hungarian convert to Islam, at a time, the reign of Ahmed III, when the empire was more open than it had been to ideas from the west. However, it printed only a handful of books, including works by the scholar-bureaucrat Katib Celebi (in 1729 and 1733), and the historian Naima (in 1734), and it did not last very long.

In the Islamic world, the fear of heresy underlay the opposition to printing and western learning. It is surely significant that Murad III allowed only non-religious books to be imported into the Ottoman Empire. Oral and manuscript communication was also subject to censorship, and the Turkish poet Nef'i was executed in 1635 for having satirized the government.

Istanbul was an important centre for performances of various kinds, including the dramatic monologues of storytellers, shadow-plays and puppet-plays. As in Europe, major events such as victories and the accession of rulers were celebrated by public festivals, many of which took place in the main public square, *At Meydani,* on the site of the Byzantine hippodrome, which survived when other public spaces were built over. The spectacles included masquerades, mock-battles, shadow-plays, floats, fireworks, dancing, juggling, and buffoonery. At other times the main centre of public performances was a district of Istanbul known as the *Tahtakalet,*. Plays could also be seen in coffee-houses, in private houses, and in the *Topkapı* palace. Indeed, some sultans were so fond of drama that they took actors with them on campaign. The actors included not only Turks but Greeks, Jews, Armenians, Egyptians and Persians (not counting the French actors who played Molière at the French embassy). Whether this variety shows that Istanbul was a cultural metropolis, a magnet for the talented, or that the city was on the periphery, dependent on foreign culture, it is difficult to say without a close analysis of the plays themselves. Even then, it is virtually impossible to decide whether parallels between the *Taklit Oyunu* and the Italian *commedia dell'arte* are due to Italian influence on the Turks, Turkish influence on the Italians, or a common heritage from Greek and Roman mime.[79]

Unlike Istanbul, Peking had relatively little contact with the world outside China, a function which was performed by Canton and other trading cities of the South.[80] However, as the capital of an empire with a population of a hundred and fifty million people in 1700 (rising to nearly three hundred million by the end of the century), it could reasonably claim to be a metropolis, and it had a rich cultural life.

Ink-painting, mainly of landscapes, was a Chinese tradition which continued to flourish in this period, whether the works were produced by professional artists or as a hobby by the literati. There were a number of regional schools, and Peking was far from dominant before the eighteenth century. However, the Qianlong emperor, who ruled from 1736 to 1795, took a great personal interest in the arts. Indeed, he is sometimes said to have "dictated" taste from Peking, since provincial elites followed his example.

China like the west possessed great libraries. The imperial library in Peking was founded in 1238, while four major libraries were constructed at the orders of the new imperial dynasty of the Qing. In the late eighteenth century, the Qianlong emperor launched an ambitious project for collecting books and bringing them to the capital. The academies too had their own libraries.

Scholars used to assume that a writing system based on ideograms rather than the alphabet prevented literacy spreading widely, on the grounds that to learn two thousand or more Chinese characters would require more years in school than ordinary people could afford for their children. Recently, however, historians have begun to stress the spread of "rudimentary literacy" in late Ming and Qing China, in other words the knowledge of relatively few characters, say a few hundred. There was a rise of relatively cheap publications around the 1570s, and various types of popular literature developed, including forms of non-fiction such as encyclopaedias and guides to letter-writing, ritual and astrology. Books such as *The Female Analects* and *The Womens' Classic of Filial Piety* were obviously intended to reach a female public.

It has also been pointed out that publishing costs were lower in China than in Europe (thanks to the dominance of a single language), so that books should have been relatively cheaper and thus accessible to more people. The Italian Jesuit Matteo Ricci, whose long stay in Peking put him in a uniquely favourable position for making comparisons with Europe, remarked on "the exceedingly large number of books in circulation" in late sixteenth-century China, and also "the ridiculously low price at which they were sold". Peking was not one of the most important cities for commercial printing, but it was the centre of official printing in this period.

In China there was a long tradition of interest in drama. Until the eighteenth century, however, plays were generally shown not in purpose-built theatres but in temples, teahouses, private houses, and at court. There were two dramatic traditions, the classical (*kunqu*), and the popular, in which acting was combined with singing, dancing and acrobatics. The eighteenth century seems to have been an important turning-point in the history of both, at least in Peking. By 1732, the actors of the city had their own guild. By 1740, the imperial househould had its own troupe of actors. In 1790, a number of regional companies came to the capital to perform in honour of the eightieth birthday of the emperor, resulting in the rise of the so-called "Peking Opera". By 1816, there were twenty-one public theatres in the capital. In this case we might reasonably speak of the "metropolitanization" of culture.[81]

In Japan, the period for which comparisons with Europe should be most fruitful is not the sixteenth century, when the country was torn by civil war, but the age of the Tokugawa shoguns, which lasted from the beginning of the seventeenth century to the middle of the nineteenth. In this period three cities were dominant: the old capital, Kyoto, still the centre of high culture as well as the residence of the emperors, who had lost power but continued to lead a secluded, ghostly existence there; Osaka, the thriving commercial centre of Japan; and Edo (now Tokyo), a small town which grew rapidly after the new dynasty had chosen it as the seat of their court.[82]

In the seventeenth century, the shogun required the presence of the leading nobles [*daimyo*] or their families in Edo, to prevent them leading rebellions in their own regions. This *sankin-kotai* system, a formalized equivalent of the strategy pursued by Louis XIV when he required the presence of the great nobles at Versailles, had important economic and cultural consequences over the long term. The presence of the *shogun* and the *daimyo* made the capital a major centre of consumption and fashion. Even more important than noble patronage, however, was the emergence of a distinctively urban popular culture as a consequence of the rapid growth of the city and the enrichment of merchants and craftsmen working for the court. This urban popular culture could also be found in Kyoto and Osaka, taking a somewhat different form in each city. Edo never quite replaced Kyoto as a centre of culture, but rather coexisted with it.

As in the case of European cities, the urban life of Japan was punctuated by regular festivals. The Sanno festival at Edo, for instance, involved the competitive construction of floats by different local groups, much like the European guilds and wards, and the procession was allowed to pass through the grounds of the castle, with the shogun looking down on the proceedings, like the doge of Venice. One of the most popular floats in the Tokugawa period represented the Korean ambassador, accompanied by an elephant to emphasize his strangeness. It has been argued that this festival helped the Japanese to define themselves by opposition to the alien Koreans, hitherto little-known.[83]

In the seventeenth century, as Kyoto, Osaka and Edo grew in size (it is likely that the latter was the largest city in the world by 1700), new types of performance emerged there, notably two types of play, the *joruri*, with puppets, and the *kabuki*, with human actors. The upper class, in other words the samurai, were not supposed to attend these performances, which were intended for ordinary people and often represented their lives (as in the case of the dramas describing couples who committed suicide because they were in love and unable to marry). In fact, all classes in the cities seem to have participated in these new forms of culture.

In the visual arts, the rise of new forms can be seen in the case of both high and low culture. Folding screens (*byobu*) were gilded and painted at great expense for the great nobles who were required to maintain a residence in the capital. A greater innovation, however, was the rise of the coloured wood-block print in the late seventeenth century (a technique borrowed from China but developed, characteristically, in an unprecedented way by the Japanese). These prints, mechanically-reproduced, and therefore cheap and so available to relatively large numbers of people, generally represented the everyday life of the city and in particular the Yoshiwara, the entertainment district of Edo. Indeed, one function of the prints was to advertise the leading actors and courtesans.[84] The texts known as *hyobanki* described the same actors and courtesans in a more critical manner. Guides to the Yoshiwara were another popular literary genre: more than two hundred of them had been published by 1700.

Japan like China had a long tradition of printing, although it was mainly confined to monasteries until the late sixteenth century. Following the invasion of Korea in 1592, the Japanese brought movable type back to Japan, and this seems to have stimulated secular printing. Like Osaka, Edo became was a major centre of printed books, not only in Chinese characters but also in the syllabic scripts (*katakana*, *hiragana*) which ordinary people and women were often able to read. By 1696 a printed catalogue published in Edo was able to list 7,800 titles arranged by subject. The so-called "Genroku era" (1688-1703) was the time when popular printed literature flourished most in the three great cities of Edo, Osaka and Kyoto. Like the new types of play, the new literary genres – from novels to guides to becoming rich – were often concerned with the everyday lives of ordinary people.[85]

Changes in Japanese learned literature were limited by the fact that the control of information became very much stricter after 1640, when the country was officially isolated from the rest of the world in reaction to the spread of Christianity. The import of foreign books dealing with Christianity or with military matters was forbidden by the government.

These restrictions began to be relaxed after 1720, however, and an interest in western science (among a small group of scholars, at least) soon became apparent, in fields ranging from surgery to astronomy (in which the ideas of Copernicus were discussed. Nagasaki, where a Dutch trading post was established, naturally became a centre of this foreign learning, but the annual visits of the Dutch to Edo helped make the capital a rival intellectual centre. The Japanese "discovery of Europe" (more exactly a rediscovery) took place long before the arrival of the famous American ships in the 1850s.[86]

# Conclusion

It is time to to sum up, to strike a balance, and to attempt to see the different cities and cultural domains described above as a whole. What makes a city a cultural metropolis? Or more precisely, what underlies the influx of artists, writers, actors and others to a particular city, thus making it more attractive to creators and consumers alike? Again and again in these pages we have observed the working of both political and economic factors.

The political factors include the presence or absence of censorship or government patronage of the arts, the whole apparatus of court painters, official printers, state-sponsored academies, and so on. The most important factor by far, however, was the rise of more and more centralized states, thus increasing the functions and consequently the size of capital cities: Rome, Madrid, Paris, London, Istanbul, Peking, Edo, and so on (one reason for the cultural decline of Antwerp, like that of Osaka, in the seventeenth century, may have been that these cities were not capitals). The growth in size of courts, located in or near major cities, led to conspicuous consumption on the arts as well as on fine clothes and banquets. The strategy of rulers concerned to cut their nobles off from their local power bases by encouraging or forcing them to live at court or in the capital increased this tendency to competitive consumption, which may sometimes have ruined the nobles concerned but gave artists a living.

Even more significant than the political changes of the sixteenth and seventeenth centuries was the process of economic growth in Europe and Asia alike, and the concomitant rise of the market, including a market in cultural goods. We have observed the rise of a market for paintings and other works of art (both contemporary art and antiques) in Rome, Venice, Antwerp, Amsterdam, Paris, and also in China and Japan. Less visible, yet operating on a much grander scale for a much wider public, was the development of the trade in books and other forms of printed matter, pamphlets, journals, newspapers, maps, prints and so on. Literature and even information were increasingly treated as commodities.

The information broker or information entrepreneur is a new but significant figure in early modern Europe. The best-known of such brokers is probably Théophraste Renaudot, founder of the Paris *Gazette* and also the *Bureau des addresses* (which arranged meetings between potential buyers and sellers, employers and employees, and so on). A similar role was played by Edward Lloyd in London.[87] Lloyd owned a coffeehouse in Lombard Street which was frequented by merchants. He founded a newspaper, *Lloyd's News,* which specialised in information about shipping. His successor's developed the maritime insurance for which Lloyd's is still known today. The regional correspondents of newspapers were another kind of information broker, including the men who followed the armies on campaign in order to be first with the news of a battle.

In a broad sense of the terms one might also describe publishers, particularly the publishers of newspapers and encyclopaedias, as buyers and sellers of information. Obvious names to mention are Elsevier of Leiden, who commissioned the famous series of volumes on the leading world states (edited by Johannes de Laet, perhaps the first intellectual to be asked to edit a series of books by different authors); Blaeuw of Amsterdam, map-maker to the Dutch East India Company and the publisher of a famous series of atlases; Leers of Rotterdam, who financed Bayle's *Dictionnaire;* Longman of London, who was the biggest shareholder in Chambers" *Cyclopaedia;* and Pancoucke of Paris, who bought the right to publish the *Encyclopédie* after its first edition.[88] It is surely no accident that seventeenth-century Amsterdam became both a leading intellectual and commercial entrepôt, a centre of publishing and news as well as a centre of trade and finance.

The rise of the market had many important consequences, not all of them desirable. In the cultural domain, it may be worth emphasising one of these consequences in particular: specialization, or the division of labour. To some degree this increasing specialization was a result of the information explosion which followed the invention of printing, to some degree a more direct result of market forces.

The French sociologist Pierre Bourdieu has recently introduced into cultural studies the notion of "field", defined as a configuration of relations which is also "a space of conflict and competition". The competition is primarily for cultural authority, in other words for a monopoly of cultural "capital".[89] Fields of this kind have emerged at various moments in European history. The literary field, for example, as Alain Viala has argued, emerged in France in the seventeenth century (largely as a result, so one might suggest, of the growth of Paris). Joseph Alsop did not use the notion of "field", but his comparative study of the art "system", already discussed above, comes to conclusions about the connections between collecting, the market, forging, and art history, from Rome to Peking, which are at the very least compatible with the ideas of Bourdieu and Viala.

At this point it may be useful to return to the parallel which was noted at the very beginning of this essay, the parallel between the sequence of the economic centres of early modern Europe as they were described by Fernand Braudel and the centres of culture in the same period. For the period 1500-1700, Braudel's sequence went from Venice to Antwerp, Genoa, and Amsterdam. Venice also makes an appropriate starting-point for a cultural sequence, given its importance as a centre of printing, painting (even if the Florentines were more innovative) and finally performance (although Venetian achievements in that area were seventeenth- rather than sixteenth-century.

Genoa, on the other hand, cannot make a very good claim to be a cultural metropolis. Although it was not, as it has sometimes been described, a city without culture, and its patricians became increasingly interested in patronage and collecting in the sixteenth and seventeenth centuries, there was no "age of the Genoese" in the arts. Amsterdam like Venice fits the Braudel model, as if economic achievements and cultural achievements are linked.

What was Antwerp's place in this cultural sequence? It was indeed an international centre of painting and printing at more or less the same time, the mid-sixteenth century, as it was a centre of international trade and finance. Some of the connexions between the economic and cultural achievements of Antwerpers have already been discussed, notably the importance of immigrants, who both created and exploited the opportunity to make the city a mediator between northern and southern Europe, especially before 1585.

One might distinguish two Antwerps, before and after the capture of the city by Parma in 1585. Before the siege, it was an outward-looking, free-thinking, cosmopolitan, independent city, the Antwerp of Pieter Coeck (who had travelled as far afield as Istanbul), of the geographer Ortelius, and of a wide range of foreign visitors from Thomas More to William Tyndale, and from Albrecht Dürer to the sceptic Henry Cornelius Agrippa. The city was a site of cultural as well as economic exchanges.

After the siege, on the other hand, what developed was a more inward-looking, orthodox society which formed part of a courtly, Catholic culture, the Antwerp of (say) Florent de Cocq, a monk and a writer on theology. "Fortress Antwerp" one might call it, the citadel of the Counter-Reformation. Rubens, of course, was cosmopolitan as well as Catholic, but his city was becoming more provincial. Readers may like to decide for themselves which Antwerp they prefer, the exchange or the fortress, and which model they would like the cultural metropolis of 1993 to follow.

# Bibliography

A.F. ALLISON AND D.M. ROGERS (1956) A Catalogue of Catholic Books in English Printed Abroad or Secretly in England, 2 vols, Bognor Regis

JOSEPH ALSOP (1982) The Rare Art Tradition, London

METIN AND (1964) A History of Theatre and Popular Entertainment in Turkey, Ankara

SYDNEY ANGLO (1969) Spectacle, Pageantry and Tudor Politics, Oxford

ROBERT ASHTON (1983) "Popular Entertainment and Social Control in Later Elizabethan and Early Stuart England", London Journal 9, 3-16

ERICH AUERBACH (1951) "La cour et la ville", English trans in his Scenes from the Drama of European Literature, New York 1959, 133-79

VIOLET BARBOUR (1950) Capitalism in Amsterdam in the 17th Century, Baltimore

H.-G. BECK (1977) Venezia Centro di mediazione tra oriente e occidente, 2 vols, Florence

A.L. BEIER AND R. FINLEY (1986) London 1500-1700: the Making of the Metropolis, London

MICHAEL BERLIN (1986) "Civic Ceremony in Early Modern London", Urban History Yearbook 15-27

PETER G. BIETENHOLZ (1959) Der italienische Humanismus und die Blütezeit des Buchdruck in Basel, Basel

PETER G. BIETENHOLZ (1971) Basle and France in the Sixteenth Century: the Basle Humanists and Printers in their Contacts with Francophone Culture, Geneva

PETER G. BIETENHOLZ (1990) "Édition et Réforme à Bâle, 1517-65", in Gilmont, 239-68

HANS BOTS (1983) "Les Provinces-Unies Centre de l'Information européenne au 17$^e$ siècle", Quaderni del "600 francese 5, 283-306

PIERRE BOURDIEU AND LOÏC J.D. WACQUANT (1992) An Invitation to Reflexive Sociology, Cambridge
FERNAND BRAUDEL (1979) Le temps du monde, Paris
J.G.C.A. BRIELS (1974) Zuidnederlandse boekdrukkers en boekverkopers in de Republiek, Nieuwkoop
GENE BRUCKER (1969) Renaissance Florence, New York
BIAGIO BRUGI (1905) Gli scolari dello studio di Padova nel '500, Padua
PETER BURKE (1974) Venice and Amsterdam, London
PETER BURKE (1992) The Fabrication of Louis XIV, New Haven and London
JAMES F. CAHILL (1982) The Compelling Image: Nature and Style in Seventeenth-Century Chinese Painting, Cambridge MA
VICENTE LLEÓ CAÑAL (1979) Nueva Roma: mitología y humanismo en el renacimiento sevillano, Seville
ENRICO CASTELNUOVO AND CARLO GINZBURG (1979) "Centro e periferia", Storia dell'arte italiana, 1, ed. Giovanni Previtali, Torino, 285-352
DAVID S. CHAMBERS (1971) The Imperial Age of Venice, London
EDMUND K. CHAMBERS (1903) The Medieval Stage, 2 vols, Oxford
ANDRÉ CHASTEL (1983) The Sack of Rome, Princeton
DAVID CHIBBETT (1977) The History of Japanese Printing and Book Illustration, Tokyo
MIRIAM U. CHRISMAN (1982) Lay culture, learned culture, New Haven
MIRIAM U. CHRISMAN (1991) "L'édition protestante à Strasbourg", in Gilmont, 217-38
COLIN CLAIR (1960) Christopher Plantin, London
ELLY COCKX-INDESTEGE AND G. GLORIEUX (1968) Belgica Typographica, Nieuwkoop
A. CORBET (1960) "L'entrée du Prince Philippe à Anvers en 1549", in Fêtes et cérémonies au temps de Charles Quint, ed. J. Jacquot, Paris, 307-10
THOMAS CROW (1985) Painters and Public Life in Eighteenth-Century Paris, Princeton
FOLKE DAHL (1939) "Amsterdam: Earliest Newspaper Centre in Western Europe", Het Boek 25, 161-97
ROBERT DARNTON (1979) The Business of Enlightenment, Cambridge, Mass., 1979
DAVID W. DAVIES (1952) "The Geographic Extent of the Dutch Book Trade in the Seventeenth Century", Library Quarterly 22, 200-13
NATALIE Z. DAVIS (1982) "Le monde de l'imprimerie humaniste: Lyon", in Histoire de l'édition française, ed. H.J. Martin and R. Chartier, Paris, 255-77

ISABELLA HENRIETTA VAN EEGHEN (1960-78) De Amsterdamse boekhandel, 1680-1725, 5 volumes in 6, Amsterdam
ROBERT J.W. EVANS (1973) Rudolf II and his World, Oxford
ZIRKA ZAREMBA FILIPCZAK (1987) Picturing Art in Antwerp 1550-1700, Princeton
F.J. FISHER (1948) "The Development of London as a Centre of Conspicuous Consumption", Transactions of the Royal Historical Society 30, 37-50
HERMAN DE LA FONTAINE VERWEYE (1962) "The Netherlands Book", in W.G. Hellinga, Copy and Print in the Netherlands, Amsterdam, 3-70
DAVID FREEDBERG (1989) The Power of Images, Chicago
GRAHAM C. GIBBS (1971) "The Role of the Dutch Republic as the Intellectual Entrepôt of Europe in the 17th and 18th Centuries", Bijdragen en Mededelingen betreffende de geschiedenis der Nederlanden 86 (1971), 323-49
J.-F. GILMONT (1990) "Trois villes frontières", in La Réforme et le livre, Paris, 187-90
G.K. GOODMAN (1967) Japan: the Dutch Experience, revised ed. London 1987
PAUL GRENDLER (1977) The Roman Inquisition and the Venetian Press, 1540-1605, Princeton
CESARE GUASTI (1884, ed) Le feste di San Giovanni Battista in Firenze, Florence
ALFRED HARBAGE (1941) Shakespeare's Audience, New York
ULF HANNERZ (1992) Cultural Complexity: Studies in the Social Organization of Meaning, New York
FRANCIS HASKELL (1960) "Art Exhibitions in Seventeenth-Century Rome", Studi secenteschi, 107-21
FRANCIS HASKELL (1963) Patrons and Painters: a Study in the Relations between Italian Art and Society in the Age of the Baroque, London, second ed. New Haven 1980
FRANCIS HASKELL AND MICHAEL LEVY (1958) "Art Exhibitions in Eighteenth-Century Venice", Arte Veneta, 12, 179-85
R.S. HATTOX (1985) Coffee and Coffee-Houses, Seattle
JULIUS HELD (1957) "An Antwerp Art Patron and his Collection", rpr his Rubens and his Circle (Princeton, 1982), 35-64
MARVIN T. HERRICK (1960) Italian Comedy in the Renaissance, Urbana
EMILE VAN HEURCK (1931) Les livres populaires flamands, Antwerp
MARSHALL HODGSON (1974) The Venture of Islam, 3: The Gunpowder Empires and Modern Times, Chicago

HALIL INALCIK (1978) "Istanbul", Encyclopaedia of Islam, new ed., IV, Leiden, 224-48

K. VAN ISACKER AND R. VAN UYTVEN (1986, eds) Antwerp: 12 centuries of history and culture, Antwerp

ROBERT M. ISHERWOOD (1986) Farce and Fantasy: Popular Entertainment in Eighteenth-Century Paris, New York

JONATHAN I. ISRAEL, "The Amsterdam Stock Exchange and the English Revolution of 1688", Tijdschrift voor Geschiedenis 103 (1990), 412-40

A.G. JOHNSTON AND J.-F. GILMONT (1990) "L'imprimerie et la réforme à Anvers", La Réforme et le livre, Paris, 191-216

EMRYS JONES (1990) Metropolis, Oxford

G. KALFF (1895) Literatuur en tooneel te Amsterdam in de 17de eeuw, Haarlem

YOSEF KAPLAN (1989) "The Portuguese Jews of Amsterdam during the Seventeenth century", in Menasseh ben Israel and his World, ed. Kaplan et al, Leiden, 45-62

THOMAS DACOSTA KAUFMANN (1985) L'école de Prague: la peinture à la cour de Rodolphe II, Paris

DONALD KEENE (1952), The Japanese Discovery of Europe

DONALD KEENE (1976) World within Walls: Japanese Literature of the Premodern Era, London

C. KOEMAN (1970) Joan Blaeuw and his Grand Atlas, London and Amsterdam

RICHARD KRAUTHEIMER (1985) The Rome of Alexander VII, Princeton

DONALD LACH (1965), Asia in the Making of Europe, Chicago

FREDERICK C. LANE (1973) Venice, a Maritime Republic, Baltimore and London

RICHARD LANE (1962), Masters of the Japanese Print, London

MICHAEL LEVEY (1975) The World of Ottoman Art, London

BERNARD LEWIS (1963) Istanbul, Norman

JOHN LOUGH (1957) Paris Theatre Audiences in the Seventeenth and Eighteenth Centuries, London

MARTIN J.C. LOWRY (1979) The World of Aldus Manutius, Oxford

M. J.C. LOWRY (1990) Nicholas Jenson and the Rise of Venetian Publishing in Renaissance Europe, Oxford

COLIN MACKERRAS (1972) The Rise of the Peking Opera (1770-1870), Oxford

NEIL MCKENDRICK, JOHN BREWER AND J.H. PLUMB (1982) The Birth of a Consumer Society: the Commercialization of Eighteenth-Century England, London

WILLIAM MCNEILL (1974) Venice the Hinge of Europe, 1081-1797, Chicago

ROBERT MANTRAN (1965) La vie quotidienne a Constantinople, Paris

H.-J. MARTIN (1984) "La prééminence de la librairie parisienne", Histoire de l'édition française 2, ed. H.-J. Martin and R. Chartier, 262-81

J.R. MARTIN (1972) The Decorations for the Pompa Introitus Ferdinandi, London and New York

N.N. MARTINOVITCH (1933) The Turkish Theatre, New York

JOHN MICHAEL MONTIAS (1982) Artists and Artisans in Delft: a Socio-Economic Study of the Seventeenth Century, Princeton

J.M. MONTIAS (1988) "Art Dealers in the Seventeenth-Century Netherlands", Simiolus 18, 244-56

EDWARD MUIR (1981) Civic Ritual in Renaissance Venice

MICHAEL NORTH (1992) Kunst und Kommerz im Goldenen Zeitalter, Cologne

PETER PARTNER (1976) Renaissance Rome, Berkeley

H.W. PEDICORD (1954) The Theatrical Public in the Time of Garrick, New York

RUTH PIKE (1966) Enterprise and Adventure: the Genoese in Seville and the Opening of the New World, Ithaca

JACK H. PLUMB (1973) The Commercialization of Leisure in Eighteenth-Century England, Reading

KEITH PRATT (1971) Peking in the Early 17th Century, Oxford

OREST RANUM (1968) Paris in the Age of Absolutism, New York

EVELYN RAWSKI (1979), Education and Popular Literacy in China, Ann Arbor

ROBERT REDFIELD AND M. SINGER (1954) "The Cultural Role of Cities", Economic Development and Cultural Change 3, 53-73

HILDA DE RIDDER-SYMOENS (1993, ed) A History of the University in Europe, volume 2, Cambridge

V. ROSSATO (1987) "Religione e moralità in un merciaio veneziano del '500", Studi Veneziani 13, 193-253

A. ROUZET (1975) Dictionnaire des imprimeurs, libraires et éditeurs des XV$^e$ et XVI$^e$ siècles dans les limites géographiques de la Belgique actuelle, Nieuwkoop

PIERRE SARDELLA (1948) Nouvelles et spéculations à Venise, Paris

JEAN SCHNAPPER (1988) "The King of France as Collector in the Seventeenth Century", in Art and History, ed. R.I. Rotberg and T.K. Rabb, Cambridge, 185-202

GARY SCHWARTZ (1985) Rembrandt, his Life, his Paintings, New York

N.D. SHERGOLD (1967) A History of the Spanish Stage, Oxford

DONALD H. SHIVELY (1991) "Popular Culture", Cambridge History of Japan 4, ed. J.W. Hall, Cambridge, 706-69

W.D. SMITH (1984) "The Function of Commercial Centres in the Modernization of European Capitalism: Amsterdam as an Information Exchange in the Seventeenth Century" Journal of Economic History 44, 985-1005

R.M. SMUTS (1991) "The Court and its Neighbourhood", Journal of British Studies 30, 117-49

HERBERT SOLOMON (1972) Public Welfare, Science and Propaganda in 17thc France, Princeton

HUGO SOLY (1986) "The Growth of a Metropolis", in Isacker, 84-92

J. VAN DER STOCK (1991, ed) Stad in Vlaanderen: Cultuur en Maatschappij 1477-1787, Brussels

GERALD STRAUSS (1967) Nuremberg in the Sixteenth Century, New York

F. SUYKENS ET AL. (1986) Antwerp: a Port for all Seasons, Antwerp

RONALD P. TOBY, "Carnival of the Aliens", Monumenta Nipponica 41 (1986) 415-56

RICHARD TREXLER (1980) Public Life in Renaissance Florence, New York

VALENTÍN VÁZQUEZ DE PRADA (1961, ed) Lettres marchandes d'Anvers, 4 vols, Paris

ALAIN VIALA (1985) Naissance de l'écrivain: sociologie de la littérature à l'âge classique, Paris

LÉON VOET (1969-72) The Golden Compasses, Amsterdam

L. VOET (1973) De gouden eeuw van Antwerpen

JAN DE VRIES (1984) European Urbanization, 1500-1800, London

MARTIN WACKERNAGEL (1938) The World of the Florentine Renaissance Artist, English translation Princeton 1981

JAMES B. WADSWORTH (1962) Lyons 1473-1503: the Beginnings of Cosmopolitanism, Cambridge MA

GARY K. WAITE (1991) "Vernacular drama and the early urban Reformation", Journal of Renaissance and Medieval Studies 21, 187-206

BURR WALLEN (1983) Jan van Hemessen: an Antwerp Painter between Reformation and Counter-Reformation, Epping

SHEILA WILLIAMS, "Les Ommegangs d'Anvers et les cortèges du Lord-Maire de Londres", in Fêtes et cérémonies au temps de Charles Quint, ed. J. Jacquot, Paris, 349-57

SHEILA WILLIAMS AND JEAN JACQUOT (1960) "Ommegangs anversois du temps de Bruegel et de van Heemskerck", in Fêtes et cérémonies au temps de Charles Quint, ed. J. Jacquot, Paris, 359-88

J.A. WORP (1908) Geschiedenis van het drama in Nederland, Groningen

SIMON T. WORSTHORNE (1954) Venetian Opera in the Seventeenth Century, Oxford

# Notes

1. F. Braudel, Le temps du monde (Paris, 1979), 71-234.
2. I. Wallerstein, The Modern World-System: Capitalist Agriculture and the Origins of the European World-Economy in the Sixteenth Century (New York, 1974).
3. Braudel, 82.
4. F.C. Lane, Venice, a Maritime Republic (Baltimore and London, 1973).
5. R. Pike, Enterprise and Adventure: the Genoese in Seville and the Opening of the New World (Ithaca, 1966).
6. V. Barbour, Capitalism in Amsterdam in the 17th Century (Baltimore, 1950).
7. P.M. Hohenberg and L.H. Lees, The Making of Urban Europe (1000-1950) (Cambridge, Mass., 1985); J. De Vries, European Urbanization 1500-1800 (London, 1984).
8. H. Soly, "The Growth of a Metropolis", in K. van Isacker and R. van Uytven, eds, Antwerp: Twelve Centuries of History and Culture (Antwerp, 1986); B. Brugi, Gli scolari dello studio di Padova nel '500 (Padua, 1905), 27.
9. D.S. Chambers, The Imperial Age of Venice (London, 1971), chapter 1; V. Lleó Cañal, Nueva Roma: mitología y humanismo en el renacimiento sevillano, (Seville, 1979); O. Ranum, Paris in the Age of Absolutism (New York, 1968).
10. E. Jones, Metropolis (Oxford, 1990), 11.
11. H. de Ridder-Symoens, ed., A History of the University in Europe, 2 (Cambridge, 1993).
12. G. Gibbs (1971) "The Role of the Dutch Republic as the Intellectual Entrepôt of Europe in the 17th and 18th Centuries", Bijdragen en Mededelingen betreffende de geschiedenis der Nederlanden 86 (1971), 323-49; Hans Bots, "Les Provinces-Unies Centre de l'Information européenne au 17$^e$ siècle", Quaderni del '600

francese 5 (1983), 283-306; W.D. Smith, "The Function of Commercial Centres in the Modernization of European Capitalism: Amsterdam as an Information Exchange in the Seventeenth Century", Journal of Economic History 44 (1984), 985-1005; J.I. Israel, "The Amsterdam Stock Exchange and the English Revolution of 1688", Tijdschrift voor Geschiedenis 103 (1990), 412-40.

13. R. Redfield and M. Singer, "The Cultural Role of Cities", Economic Development and Cultural Change 3 (1954), 53-73.

14. E. Castelnuovo and C. Ginzburg, "Centro e periferia", Storia dell'arte italiana 1, ed. G. Previtali (Torino, 1979), 285-352.

15. M. Wackernagel, The World of the Florentine Renaissance Artist (1938: English translation, Princeton 1981), 300. For a general view of the city, see G. Brucker, Renaissance Florence (New York, 1969).

16. Wackernagel; Joseph Alsop, The Rare Art Tradition (London, 1982), 444.

17. D. Beltrami, Storia della popolazione di Venexia dalla fine del secolo XVI alla caduta Repubblica (Padua, 1954), 208. On Venice more generally, F.C. Lane, Venice, a Maritime Republic (Baltimore, 1973).

18. D. Howard, Jacopo Sansovino: Architecture and Patronage in Renaissance Venice (New Haven, 1975).

19. Alsop, 96, 149-50; F. Haskell and M. Levy, "Art Exhibitions in Eighteenth-Century Venice", Arte Veneta 12 (1958), 179-85.

20. P. Partner, Renaissance Rome (Berkeley and Los Angeles, 1976), 92; A. Chastel, The Sack of Rome (Princeton, 1983).

21. Alsop, 158; F. Haskell, "Art Exhibitions in Seventeenth-Century Rome", Studi secenteschi (1960), 107-21; id, Patrons and Painters: a Study in the Relations between Italian Art and Society in the Age of the Baroque (London, 1963: second ed, New Haven 1980).

22. Alsop.

23. G. Strauss, Nuremberg in the Sixteenth Century (New York, 1967).

24. R.J.W. Evans, Rudolf II and his World (Oxford, 1973), especially chapter 5; T. DaCosta Kaufmann, L'école de Prague: la peinture à la cour de Rodolphe II (Paris, 1985).

25. Z.Z. Filipczak, Picturing Art in Antwerp 1550-1700 (Princeton, 1987), 3, 21, 55.

26. B. Wallen, Jan van Hemessen: an Antwerp Painter between Reformation and Counter-Reformation (Epping, 1983).

27. J.S. Held, "An Antwerp Art Patron and his Collection", rpr in his Rubens and his Circle (Princeton, 1982), 35-64.

28. On art patronage in Amsterdam, P. Burke, Venice and Amsterdam (London, 1974), ch. 8; G. Schwartz, Rembrandt, his Life, his Paintings (New York, 1985).
29. J.M. Montias, "Art Dealers in the Seventeenth-Century Netherlands", Simiolus 18 (1988), 244-56; M. North, Kunst und Kommerz im Goldenen Zeitalter (Cologne, 1992).
30. J.M. Montias, Artists and Artisans in Delft: a Socio-Economic Study of the Seventeenth Century (Princeton, 1982).
31. J. Schnapper, "The King of France as Collector in the Seventeenth Century", in Art and History, ed. R.I. Rotberg and T.K. Rabb. (Cambridge, 1988), 185-202; P. Burke, The Fabrication of Louis XIV (New Haven and London, 1992); T. Crow, Painters and Public Life in Eighteenth-Century Paris (Princeton, 1985).
32. Alsop, 151.
33. C. Guasti, Le feste di San Giovanni Battista in Firenze (Florence, 1884); R. Trexler, Public Life in Renaissance Florence (New York, 1980).
34. E. Muir, Civic Ritual in Renaissance Venice (Princeton, 1981).
35. P. Burke, "The Carnival of Venice", in Historical Anthropology of Early Modern Italy (Cambridge, 1987), 183-90.
36. S. Anglo, Spectacle, Pageantry and Early Tudor Policy (Oxford, 1969), 170-206.
37. M. Berlin, "Civic Ceremony in Early Modern London", Urban History Yearbook (1986) 15-27.
38. E.K. Chambers, The Medieval Stage (2 vols, Oxford, 1903).
39. M.T. Herrick, Italian Comedy in the Renaissance (Urbana, 1960).
40. On the idea of "critical mass" in cultural change, see U. Hannerz, Cultural Complexity: Studies in the Social Organization of Meaning (New York, 1992), 201.
41. J. Lough, Paris Theatre Audiences in the Seventeenth and Eighteenth Centuries (London, 1957); S.T. Worsthorne, Venetian Opera in the Seventeenth Century (Oxford, 1954).
42. N.D. Shergold, A History of the Spanish Stage (Oxford, 1967).
43. F.J. Fisher, "The Development of London as a Centre of Conspicuous Consumption", Transactions of the Royal Historical Society 30 (1948), 37-50; A.L. Beier and R. Finley, eds, London 1500-1700: the Making of the Metropolis (London, 1986).
44. A. Harbage, Shakespeare's Audience (New York, 1941), 91; R. Ashton, "Popular Entertainment and Social Control in Later Elizabethan and Early Stuart England", London Journal 9 (1983), 3-16.
45. H.W. Pedicord, The Theatrical Public in the Time of Garrick (New York, 1954).

46. J. Lough, Paris Theatre Audiences in the Seventeenth and Eighteenth Centuries (London, 1957).
47. G.K. Waite, "Vernacular Drama and the Early Urban Reformation: the Chambers of Rhetoric in Amsterdam, 1520-50", Journal of Medieval and Renaissance Studies 21 (1991), 187-206.
48. G. Kalff, Literatuur en tooneel te Amsterdam in de 17de eeuw (Haarlem, 1895); J.A. Worp, Geschiedenis van het drama in Nederland (Groningen, 1908).
49. S. Williams, "Les ommegangs d'Anvers", in Fêtes et Cérémonies au temps de Charles Quint, ed. J. Jacquot (Paris, 1960), 349-57.
50. A. Corbet, "L'entrée du Prince Philippe à Anvers en 1549", in Jacquot, 307-10; J.R. Martin, The Pompa Introitus Ferdinandi (London & New York, 1972)
51. J.H. Plumb, The Commercialization of Leisure in Eighteenth-Century England (Reading, 1973); N. McKendrick, J. Brewer and J.H. Plumb, The Birth of a Consumer Society: the Commercialization of Eighteenth-Century England (London, 1982).
52. R.M. Isherwood, Farce and Fantasy: Popular Entertainment in Eighteenth-Century Paris (New York, 1986).
53. The figures are derived from the short-title catalogues published by the Library.
54. H.-G. Beck, ed., Venezia centro di mediazione tra oriente e occidente (2 vols, Florence 1977); W.H. McNeill, Venice the Hinge of Europe, 1081-1797 (Chicago, 1974); P. Sardella, Nouvelles et spéculations à Venise (Paris, 1948).
55. M.J.C. Lowry, The World of Aldus Manutius (Oxford, 1979); id, Nicholas Jenson and the Rise of Venetian Publishing in Renaissance Europe (Oxford, 1990).
56. P. Grendler, The Roman Inquisition and the Venetian Press, 1540-1605 (Princeton, 1977).
57. V. Rossati, "Religione e moralità in un merciaio veneziano del '500", Studi Veneziani 13 (1987), 193-253.
58. N.Z. Davies, "le monde de l'imprimerie humaniste: Lyon", in Histoire de l'édition française, ed. H. - J. Martin and R. Chartier, 1 (Paris, 1982), 255-77.
59. J.-F. Gilmont, "Trois villes frontières: Anvers, Strasbourg et Bâle", in La réforme et le livre, ed. Gilmont (Paris, 1990), 191-216.
60. P.G. Bietenholz, Der italienische Humanismus und die Blütezeit des Buchdruck in Basel (Basel, 1959); P.G. Bietenholz (1971) Basle and France in the Sixteenth Century: the Basle Humanists and Printers in their Contacts with Francophone Culture (Geneva, 1971);

P.G. Bietenholz (1990) "Édition et Réforme à Bâle, 1517-65", in Gilmont, 239-68; M.U. Chrisman, Lay Culture, Learned Culture (New Haven, 1982).
61. C. Clair, Christopher Plantin (London, 1960); L. Voet, The Golden Compasses (2 vols, Amsterdam 1969-72).
62. E. Cockx-Indestege and G. Glorieux, Belgica Typographica (Nieuwkoop, 1968).
63. A.G. Johnston and J.-F. Gilmont, "L'imprimerie et la réforme à Anvers", in La réforme et le livre, ed. Gilmont (Paris, 1990), 191-216.
64. W. Nijhoff and M.E. Kronenberg, Nederlandsche Bibliographie (The Hague, 1923).
65. A. Rouzet, Dictionnaire des imprimeurs, libraires et éditeurs des XV$^e$ et XVI$^e$ siècles dans les limites géographiques de la Belgique actuelle (Nieuwkoop, 1975), 163.
66. J.F. Cahill, The Compelling Image: Nature and Style in Seventeenth-Century Chinese Painting (Cambridge, Mass., 1982), 75.
67. A.F. Allison and D.M. Rogers, The Contemporary Literature of the English Counter-Reformation (Aldershot, 1989).
68. E.H. van Heurck, Les livres populaires flamands (Antwerp, 1931).
69. E. Auerbach, "La cour et la ville", English trans in his Scenes from the Drama of European Literature (New York, 1959), 133-79.
70. C. Koeman, Joan Blaeuw and his Grand Atlas (London and Amsterdam, 1970).
71. I.H. van Eeghen, De Amsterdamse boekhandel, 1680-1725 (5 volumes in 6, Amsterdam 1960-78).
72. D.W. Davies, "The Geographic Extent of the Dutch Book Trade in the Seventeenth Century", Library Quarterly 22 (1952), 200-13.
73. W.P.C. Knuttel, ed., Catalogus van de Pamfletten Verzameling Berustende in de Koninklike Bibliotheek (9 volumes, The Hague 1889-1920).
74. F. Dahl, "Amsterdam: Earliest Newspaper Centre in Western Europe", Het Boek 25 (1939), 161-97.
75. H. Bots, "Les Provinces-Unies centre de l'information europénne au dix-septième siècle", Quaderni del '600 francese 5 (1983), 283-306; G.C. Gibbs, "The Role of the Dutch Republic as the Intellectual Entrepôt of Europe in the Seventeenth and Eighteenth Centuries", Bijdragen en Mededelingen betreffende de geschiedenis der Nederlanden 86 (1971), 323-49; W.D. Smith, "The Function of Commercial Centres in the Modernisation of Capitalism: Amsterdam as an Information Exchange in the Seventeenth Century", Journal of Economic History 44 (1984), 985-1005.

76. B. Lewis, Istanbul (Norman, 1963); R. Mantran, La vie quotidienne à Constantinople (Paris, 1965); Halil Inalcik (1978) "Istanbul", Encyclopaedia of Islam, new ed., IV, Leiden, 224-48

77. M. Levey, The World of Ottoman Art (London, 1975).

78. M. Hodgson, The Venture of Islam, 3: The Gunpowder Empires and Modern Times (Chicago, 1974).

79. N.N. Martinovitch, The Turkish Theatre (New York, 1933); M. And, A History of Theatre and Popular Entertainment in Turkey (Ankara, 1964).

80. M. Elvin, "Chinese Cities" in P. Abrams & E.A. Wrizley, in Towns in Societies (Cambridge, 1978); C. Mackerras, The Rise of the Peking Opera; K. Pratt, Peking in the Early 17th Century (Oxford 1971).

81. C. Mackerras, The Rise of the Peking Opera (1770-1870) (Oxford, 1972).

82. J.W. Hall, ed. Early Modern Japan (Cambridge, 1991).

83. R.P. Toby, "Carnival of the Aliens", Monumenta Nipponica 41 (1986) 415-56.

84. R. Lane, Masters of the Japanese Print (London, 1962).

85. D. Chibbett, The History of Japanese Printing and Book Illustration (Tokyo 1977); D.H. Shively, "Popular Culture", Cambridge History of Japan 4, ed. J.W. Hall (Cambridge, 1991), 706-69.

86. D. Keene, The Japanese Discovery of Europe (London, 1952); G.K. Goodman, Japan: the Dutch Experience (revised ed., London 1987).

87. H. Solomon, Public Welfare, Science and Propaganda in Seventeenth-Century France, (Princeton, 1972).

88. R. Darnton, The Business of Enlightenment, (Cambridge, Mass., 1979).

89. P. Bourdieu and L.J.D. Wacquant, An Invitation to Reflexive Sociology (Cambridge, 1992), 17.

*Publishing, design and printing:*
Snoeck-Ducaju & Zoon

*Cover design:*
Bernard Van Eeghem

ISBN 90-5349-059-0
D/1993/0012/5